Inheritance
and the State

Inheritance and the State

Tax Principles for a Free and Prosperous Commonwealth

Richard E. Wagner

American Enterprise Institute for Public Policy Research
Washington, D.C.

Richard E. Wagner is professor of economics at Virginia Polytechnic Institute and State University.

AEI Studies 154

Library of Congress Cataloging in Publication Data

Wagner, Richard E
  Inheritance and the state.

  (AEI studies ; 154)
  Includes bibliographical references.
  1. Inheritance and transfer tax—United States.
I. Title. II. Series: American Enterprise Institute
for Public Policy Research. AEI studies ; 154.
HJ5805.W253   336.2'76'0973   77-8549
ISBN O-8447-3252-4

Printed in the United States of America

CONTENTS

INTRODUCTION

A time to die is also a time to be taxed, at least under prevailing customs, provided the decedent leaves behind more than the proverbial handful of dust. It is possible that some time in the future death will not inspire the tax collectors so. But this is the custom for the present, the changes promulgated in the Tax Reform Act of 1976 notwithstanding.

There have been periods in our history when inheritance taxes did not exist. There were none before the Stamp Act of 1797, and with the repeal of that act in 1802 we reverted to our former ways. Except for brief interludes during both the Civil War and the Spanish-American War, death did not imply taxation until 1916. Since then, death has been a green light to the tax collectors, although there was a period during the 1920s when this new custom seemed in jeopardy. The New Deal erased those fears.

State governments have also seen fit to tax transfers of wealth, though their take is but a pittance in comparison with that of the federal government. Pennsylvania led the way in 1825, and all of the states have followed suit except Nevada. The federal government, it should be noted, has strongly encouraged the states in this activity by offering them sizable subsidies for the imposition of such taxes.

Before the Tax Reform Act of 1976 (P.L. 94–455), which largely enacted modifications of proposals introduced by the Treasury De-

I should like to acknowledge my gratitude to several persons who read and commented on a draft version of this volume: Professor Oswald Brownlee of the University of Minnesota, Professor James M. Buchanan of Virginia Polytechnic Institute and State University, Dr. Gary C. Hufbauer of the U.S. Treasury Department; Professor Dan Throop Smith of the Hoover Institution, Professor Robert J. Staaf of Virginia Polytechnic Institute and State University, and Professor Leland B. Yeager of the University of Virginia.

partment in 1969, the system of federal taxation of wealth transfers had been essentially the same for approximately a generation.[1] The 1976 act introduced several particular changes. The separate taxation of estates and gifts was replaced by a unified tax on wealth transfers. The personal exemption was increased, as was the marital deduction, and several other changes were made. The recent interest in the taxation of wealth transfers, of which the 1976 act is one manifestation, along with an awareness that it is possible for legislation to reflect an inadequate understanding of the nature of the phenomena it deals with, motivates this examination of the conceptual foundations and empirical practices of transfer taxation.

Any proposal for tax revision will, in comparison with the status quo or with other possible revisions, entail a shift in the amounts extracted by government from different persons. A shift from a proportional income tax to a progressive income tax of equal yield will alter the structure of personal tax payments by increasing payments made by those in the upper income ranges and lowering payments made by those in the lower income ranges. Similarly, a shift from a proportional tax on income to a proportional tax on net wealth will alter the structure of tax payments; because wealth is distributed less equally than income, this shift would further increase the tax extractions from those in the upper income ranges while reducing those from persons in the lower income ranges. Indeed, one of the primary rationales advanced for the taxation of transfers of wealth has been the desire to use such taxation to reduce the extent of inequality in the ownership of wealth and to do so by paring down the wealth of those in the relatively high levels.[2]

Besides influencing the distribution of income and wealth among persons, a tax also captures revenue for the state.[3] The choice of one revenue form over another will also influence the operation of the

---

[1] The existing system of taxing wealth transfers is described in the appendix to this volume. For the 1969 proposals, see U.S. Treasury Department, *Tax Reform Studies and Proposals* (Washington, D.C.: 1969).

[2] Gerard M. Brannon, "Death Taxes in a Structure of Progressive Taxes," *National Tax Journal*, vol. 26 (September 1973), pp. 451-57; Vasco N. P. Fortuna, "The Sociometric Theory and the Estate Duty," *Public Finance*, vol. 6, no. 3 (1951), pp. 267-71; and Alan A. Tait, "The Taxation of Wealth at Death: A New Proposal," *Scottish Journal of Political Economy*, vol. 9 (February 1962), pp. 38-45.

[3] Estimated federal estate and gift tax collections for fiscal 1975 were $6 billion, and collections by state governments were $1.4 billion. In each case the amount was less than 2 percent of total tax collections by the respective levels of government. See *Facts and Figures on Government Finance*, 18th ed. (New York: Tax Foundation, Inc., 1975), pp. 99 and 184-85 respectively.

economic order. By influencing the returns to different types of activities, taxes will generally influence the structure of market activity.[4] Taxes on personal income, for instance, will influence a person's choice between work and leisure. Such a tax will also influence the choice among occupations which differ in the relative amounts of monetary and nonmonetary rewards they offer. A tax on saving or wealth will influence the choice between consumption and saving by penalizing the latter relative to the former. So will taxes on consumption, only in reverse. Changes in taxation will also generally influence the fiscal activities of the state. By changing the shares of the total tax burden borne by different persons and groups, tax institutions can influence the reactions of citizens to different budget sizes.[5] Shifts in tax institutions can also influence the knowledge that citizens possess concerning the real burden to them of the activities of the state, thereby also affecting citizen reactions to fiscal and political choices.[6] These various ways in which taxes can influence the economic order provide a basis not only for assessing the impact of different tax forms and proposals for revision but also for understanding the various reactions, private and public, to different tax forms.

My examination of transfer taxation proceeds in three stages. Chapter 1, the first of two chapters on some important intellectual underpinnings, takes account of the function of inheritance in providing for future generations and, by implication, the impact of transfer taxation upon the future. Chapter 2 explores the egalitarian imperative that so thoroughly pervades contemporary discussion. Chapter 3, the first of four chapters on particular points of contention, appraises the tax treatment of capital gains that are unrealized upon death. Chapter 4 examines the relation between transfer taxation and the private support of philanthropic activity, while Chapter 5 analyzes the impact of inflation upon the real burden of transfer taxation over time. Chapter 6 delves into several special issues: the marital deduction, the impact of transfer taxation upon closely held businesses, the use of trusts, and the concurrent taxation of transfers of wealth by the federal government and by forty-nine of the state governments.

---

[4] For a thorough examination of this property of taxation, see Richard A. Musgrave, *The Theory of Public Finance* (New York: McGraw-Hill, 1959), pp. 205-401.

[5] James M. Buchanan, *Public Finance in Democratic Process* (Chapel Hill: University of North Carolina Press, 1967).

[6] Richard E. Wagner, "Revenue Structure, Fiscal Illusion, and Budgetary Choice," *Public Choice*, vol. 24 (Spring 1976), pp. 45-61.

Chapter 7, the first of two final chapters relating the previous analytical points to some matters of principle, investigates three alternative principles that have been advanced to guide the taxation of wealth transfers. Chapter 8 concludes by summarizing the implications of the preceding analysis for revision of our system of taxing transfers of wealth.[7] The appendix describes the present institutional framework for taxing transfers of wealth.

In 1973 the American Enterprise Institute published a small monograph of mine, *Death and Taxes: Some Perspectives on Inheritance, Inequality, and Progressive Taxation*. In large measure, I regard the present volume as superseding *Death and Taxes*. A few topics examined there are not considered here, while in a few other cases material from that monograph is reproduced here. For the most part, however, this volume contains both a more extensive treatment of topics covered in *Death and Taxes* and an expansion of coverage to include topics not treated there. In addition, this volume is somewhat different in perspective, reflecting the refinement in my own thinking that has taken place over the past four years.

---

[7] For a sample of surveys on reform of our system of transfer taxation, see John H. Alexander, "Federal Estate and Gift Taxation: The Major Issues Presented in the American Law Institute Project," *Tax Law Review*, vol. 22 (May 1967), pp. 635-84; A. James Casner, "American Law Institute Federal Estate and Gift Tax Project," *Tax Law Review*, vol. 22 (May 1967), pp. 515-87; Richard B. Covey, "Estate and Gift Taxation: Canadian and U.S. Systems and Proposals for Change," *1973 Proceedings of the National Tax Association* (Columbus, Ohio: National Tax Association, 1974), pp. 160-94; Marvin K. Collie, "Estate and Gift Tax Revision," *National Tax Journal*, vol. 26 (September 1973), pp. 441-49; Janet M. Mieburger, "Current Suggestions for Gift and Estate Tax Legislation," *Tax Law Review*, vol. 30 (Spring 1975), pp. 451-64; Joseph A. Pechman, *Federal Tax Policy*, rev. ed. (Washington, D.C.: Brookings Institution, 1971), pp. 185-210; and Carl S. Shoup, *Federal Estate and Gift Taxes* (Washington, D.C.: Brookings Institution, 1966).

1

INHERITANCE AND FUTURE GENERATIONS

One primary impetus for imposing taxes upon the occasion of a person's death has been, as we shall see in Chapter 2, the desire to reduce the degree of inequality in the distribution of wealth. But the taxation of wealth transfers also diminishes the incentive to accumulate capital to pass on to heirs. In consequence, the productive capacity of the nation is lowered, and, moreover, the character of the social order as it evolves historically may be modified. These long-term consequences are the subject of this chapter.

Saving in the Economic Process

The importance of saving in promoting our material well-being is not as well appreciated as it once was or as it might be. We seem to have lost sight of it for several reasons. While production was once regarded as the most important problem of economic life, distribution has assumed this position during the past century. Much credit or blame for the articulation of this view must go to John Stuart Mill, who, breaking sharply with Adam Smith, argued that the conditions governing distribution were utterly distinct from the conditions governing production. While Mill regarded the latter conditions as technical or natural and hence unchangeable, he regarded the former conditions as man-made and hence subject to human control. His perspective suggests that one can bring about nearly any distribution of output one chooses and can do so without substantially modifying the amount of production.

There seems to be little doubt that the increasing emphasis on distribution as the focal point of economic life has had detrimental consequences for production. A variety of tax practices, for instance, operate to penalize saving and investment, while at the same time encouraging consumption and promoting a redistribution of economic output.[1] The so-called paradox of thrift has also contributed to the shift in emphasis from production and saving to distribution and consumption. This thesis holds that a market economy is always in danger of generating too much saving, with the end result being recession or depression. Because saving decisions and investment decisions are made by separate individuals acting independently of one another, according to this view there is no assurance that the two magnitudes will balance. And if they do not, particularly if the savers save more than the investors invest, the volume of spending will be insufficient to absorb what the economy is capable of producing. Within the framework of neo-Keynesian economics, this excessive saving will bring about a fall in national income, a recession, or even a depression. An expansion in saving, in other words, can pave the way to the poorhouse. Conversely, the road to riches lies in spending, not saving. Benjamin Franklin's ode to penny-pinching notwithstanding, we are now told that spending is the way to wealth and saving is the way to poverty. The paradox of thrift suggests that what is prudence for one is folly for all and, conversely, what is folly for one is prudence for all.[2]

The paradox of thrift might seem to have a superficial plausibility. If people were suddenly to increase their saving and were to do so by storing part of their money balances in coffee cans in their attics, the lower rate of spending would depress business activity. This depression would continue until nominal prices and wages declined sufficiently to restore an appropriate pattern of real prices and wages. In this case, saving reduces the nominal quantity of money in circulation, and this contraction depresses the state of business activity. If the structure of wages and prices is rigid, monetary contraction must have a depressant effect. But saving itself is not depressive, for it represents not a decline in spending but merely a shift in spending

---

[1] For discussions of such tax practices, see, for instance, Joel Barlow, "The Tax Law Bias Against Investment in Production Facilities," *National Tax Journal*, vol. 26 (September 1973), pp. 415-37; Carl H. Madden, "Is Our Tax System Making Us Second-Rate?" *National Tax Journal*, vol. 26 (September 1973), pp. 403-7; and Norman B. Ture, "Capital Needs, Profits, and Inflation," *Tax Review*, vol. 36 (January 1975), pp. 1-4.

[2] The paradox of thrift, enunciated by John Maynard Keynes, has found its way into many texts and informs much journalistic commentary and popular belief. For a recent book devoted to the theme that "saving becomes relatively too high, and spending relatively too low" (p. 3), see Leon H. Keyserling, *The Scarcity School of Economics* (Washington, D.C.: Conference on Economic Progress, 1973).

from the production of consumer goods to the production of capital goods.[3]

Conversely, by spending more and saving less, an individual can certainly consume at a higher level than otherwise—for a while. In the long run, however, his increased spending for consumption could be made possible only by capital consumption.[4] While capital consumption permits higher rates of consumption in the immediate situation, it lowers the rate of consumption that is ultimately sustainable. Benjamin Franklin was right all along: the penny pincher, not the spendthrift, holds the key to economic progress.[5]

Crusonia Plants and Fishing Spears

The widespread belief that spending is the way to prosperity has undoubtedly contributed to a policy mix that discourages saving and investment. Another factor that has played a part in deemphasizing saving is the notion that capital, once created, is permanent. According to this view, the yield from capital creates the very conditions necessary for the maintenance and replacement of the capital. That is, the increased production made possible by the more capital-intensive form of production can be devoted in part to the maintenance and replacement of the capital when required. In consequence, according to this model, the maintenance of a capital stock is virtually automatic.

The parable of the Crusonia plant has long been used to illustrate the permanence of capital and the corresponding perspective on the economic order. Suppose that a Crusonia plant weighs 100 pounds and grows at an annual rate of 10 percent. This plant provides a *permanent* rate of consumption of 10 pounds annually. Should less than 10 pounds be consumed in any given year, the plant would

---

[3] For a recent argument demolishing the paradox of thrift, see W. H. Hutt, *A Rehabilitation of Say's Law* (Athens, Ohio: Ohio University Press, 1974).

[4] Capital consumption, in an opportunity-cost sense, need not imply an absolute reduction in the capital stock. A relative reduction in the capital stock from what it might have been is also capital consumption. On the general principle underlying this point, see James M. Buchanan, *Cost and Choice* (Chicago: Markham, 1969).

[5] For an interesting discussion along these lines, see Fritz Machlup, "The Consumption of Capital in Austria," *Review of Economics and Statistics*, vol. 17 (January 1935), pp. 13-19. For a thorough examination of the paradox of thrift in relation to recent controversies over the role of saving and capital in the economic process, see Leland B. Yeager, "Toward Understanding Some Paradoxes in Capital Theory," *Economic Inquiry*, vol. 14 (September 1976), pp. 313-46.

weigh more than 100 pounds at the end of the year and the possible permanent rate of consumption would rise above 10 pounds. Consumption of only 5 pounds, for instance, would increase the size of the plant to 105 pounds, thereby increasing the subsequent sustainable yield to 10.5 pounds. Conversely, an expansion in consumption beyond 10 pounds in a particular year would reduce the size of the plant below 100 pounds, thereby reducing the sustainable annual yield below 10 pounds.[6]

The key concept here is the permanent or automatically self-perpetuating character of economic output. Every act of saving and investment can be regarded as expanding *in perpetuity* the stream of economic output. The additional five pounds of plant saved and invested in one particular year increase annual output by one-half pound each year in perpetuity. This perspective fits nicely with Mill's separation between production and distribution. Production essentially creates no problem, for it is perpetual. Adoption of this perspective toward the economic order would seem to lead quite readily toward an emphasis on the distribution of income and wealth as the primary sources of concern for the functioning of the economic order. With production essentially assured, distribution becomes the object of the more intense concern.[7]

Fishing spears have also been used to illustrate the essential character of the economic process, though to convey a quite different perspective on the economic order. In this alternative perspective, the emphasis is on the essential impermanence of capital in the absence of contravening acts of human choice.[8] The fishing spear metaphor goes like this: A man lives by fishing. He can catch fish by hand or, alternatively, he can first construct a fishing spear and then use the spear to assist him in catching fish. In this case, he will spend less time fishing because some of his time is devoted to constructing the spear, but he is willing to postpone consumption while the spear is

---

[6] For a systematic presentation of this perspective, see Donald Dewey, *Modern Capital Theory* (New York: Columbia University Press, 1965). For a classic statement of this perspective, see Frank H. Knight, "Diminishing Returns from Investment," *Journal of Political Economy*, vol. 52 (March 1944), pp. 26-47.

[7] While the Crusonia plant metaphor was used by Frank Knight to illustrate his approach to capital and interest, Friedrich Lutz suggests that the particular features of a zero period of production and the view that capital is essentially permanent cannot be fitted sensibly within Knight's overall view of the economic process. See Friedrich A. Lutz, *The Theory of Interest* (Chicago: Aldine, 1968), pp. 104-23.

[8] For a survey of these alternative positions, see Israel Kirzner, *An Essay on Capital* (New York: Kelley, 1966), esp. pp. 55-64.

being constructed because of his anticipation of a higher yield. Suppose that 1,000 pounds of fish are caught annually by hand. Further suppose that 1,100 pounds of fish can be caught in eleven months with the spear, it being assumed that construction of the spear requires one month and that the spear must be replaced after eleven months of use. The spear, then, requires a one-month delay before fishing can commence. It is anticipated that, figuratively speaking, approximately 83 pounds of fish can be transformed into the spear over the month and will then maintain that form for eleven months. In exchange, total catch over the year will increase by 100 pounds. It could be said that the rate of return on the one-month's worth of labor stored up in the spear was in excess of 100 percent. And it could be said that the process could be repeated at the end of the year when the spear wore out. In this manner, the process could be repeated in perpetuity. The fishing spear becomes, as it were, an 83-pound fish growing at an annual rate in excess of 100 percent.

The implications of the Crusonia plant and the fishing spear metaphors appear identical because their static equilibrium properties are identical.[9] The differences in emphasis, however, are very important.[10] The fishing spear does not automatically reproduce itself. It is always in the process of wearing out, and its replacement requires conscious planning. If there are to be spears, decisions must continually be made as to whether to postpone consumption. It is the decision to abstain from present consumption that makes possible the creation of the fishing spear that will increase future consumption.

The process of saving and investing makes it possible for labor to be stored in specific form for future use; the construction of a fishing spear is a way of saving labor for use in the future. Producing with capital goods puts one nearer in time to enjoyment of the final output than producing without capital goods. The fishing spear makes it possible to consume the eleven-hundredth pound of fish after twelve months, whereas it would have taken longer than thirteen

---

[9] An alternative interpretation might be that the Crusonia plant is a reduction of the fishing spear, metaphorically speaking—and a reduction need not impair understanding so long as the reduction is recognized for what it is. A *Classics Illustrated* version of Dostoevski or Dickens may be fine as long as the originals are read as well. But this would not be so if the originals came to be replaced by the reductions. And so it would seem with Crusonia plants and fishing spears.

[10] For a survey of these differences as they have appeared in the history of capital theory, with the adherents of the Crusonia plant approach being referred to as materialists and the adherents of the fishing spear approach being referred to as fundists, see John R. Hicks, "Capital Controversies: Ancient and Modern," *American Economic Review*, Proceedings, vol. 64 (May 1974), pp. 307-16.

months to do this without the spear. An increase in capital, which takes place through saving and investment, is an increase in the amount of stored-up labor that is available for use in the production process. It expands the sustainable output of consumer goods.

Capital is not automatically self-perpetuating, so neither is output or consumption. Rather, automatic depreciation is the rule. This depreciation of productive capacity cannot be prevented, but it can be offset by conscious action to postpone consumption by saving and investing. By saving one can escape a hand-to-mouth existence. The natural order of an economy is not high-level consumption, but subsistence. Just as nature will ultimately devour even the stateliest of mansions unless offsetting effort is expended, so the productive capacity of a social order will contract in the absence of conscious effort to maintain and expand it.

The primary social problem is not distributing the output from some perpetually growing Crusonia plant, but abstaining, saving, even to maintain, let alone improve, the material conditions of life. It is saving and capital formation, in conjunction with knowledge, that make such improvement possible. Saving makes capital accumulation, the storing up of labor in specific form, possible. The future output that will be produced by this stored up labor depends, in turn, upon the knowledge that exists concerning both different means of storing up labor in specific form and different uses for such labor. Developing a fork to replace a spear would be one suitable illustration. It is the savers or the accumulators who are the chief benefactors of society, for by their postponement of consumption they contribute to the advancement of the material conditions of life for all. Ludwig von Mises has put this point as well as anyone:

> Every single performance in this ceaseless pursuit of wealth production is based upon the saving and the preparatory work of earlier generations. We are the lucky heirs of our fathers and forefathers whose saving has accumulated the capital goods with the aid of which we are working today. We favorite children of the age of electricity still derive advantage from the original saving of the primitive fishermen who, in producing the first nets and canoes, devoted a part of their working time to provision for a remoter future. If the sons of these legendary fishermen had worn out these intermediary products—nets and canoes—without replacing them by new ones, they would have consumed capital and the process of saving and capital accumulation would have

had to start afresh. We are better off than earlier generations because we are equipped with the capital goods they have accumulated for us.[11]

Capital Taxation, Income Taxation, and Death

The taxation of wealth has received much support as a means of raising revenue. Are there reasonable grounds for suggesting that a tax on wealth or net worth could either substitute for income taxation or complement it?[12] If this question is answered affirmatively, we must ask then whether we can look upon the taxation of wealth transferred at death as a convenient substitute for an annual tax on net worth. A commonly espoused principle, for instance, has been that wealth should be taxed once a generation so as to offset an imagined cumulative inequality, and some have suggested that estate taxation is a natural means of accomplishing this objective.

In principle, of course, a wealth tax is indistinguishable from an income tax, for any income flow can be assigned an equivalent capital value. If an asset yields an annual net income of $10,000 and if the rate of interest is 10 percent, the value of the asset will be $100,000. An annual tax of 10 percent of the net income generated by the asset would be identical to an annual tax of 1 percent on the value of the asset. A capital value is a present value of an anticipated future income stream, so income taxation at t percent would be equivalent to capital taxation at tr percent, where r is the rate of interest. This identity of income and capital taxation would seem to suggest that only one of the two bases should be used, for to combine elements of both in the same tax system would be to create instances of double taxation.

In practice, however, the base of a capital tax differs from that of an income tax. Under the personal income tax, the cost of maintaining physical capital is an expense that is deductible in computing the net taxable income from that asset. Human beings, however, are not allowed to deduct the cost of maintaining their human capital in determining their tax liability. This pair of observations prompts the argument that the income tax discriminates against human capital relative to physical capital and encourages the suggestion that a net-

---

[11] Ludwig von Mises, *Human Action*, 3rd ed. (Chicago: Henry Regnery, 1966), p. 492.

[12] For an affirmative answer, see Alan A. Tait, *The Taxation of Personal Wealth* (Urbana, Ill.: University of Illinois Press, 1967), pp. 19-21.

worth tax should be adopted to create an offsetting discrimination against physical capital. If this line of argument is correct, the adoption of a net-worth tax to complement the income tax would be a means both for restoring equity between human and nonhuman sources of wealth and for promoting an efficient allocation of resources between human and nonhuman forms of wealth.[13]

It has also been suggested that the ownership of capital goods is an additional source of tax-paying capacity. Income, it is suggested, does not fully reflect the relative capacities of different people. The reason is that they may own different amounts of wealth, of physical capital. Between two people with equal incomes, but of whom one owns more physical capital than the other, this line of argument would suggest that the one with the larger value of physical capital should be taxed more heavily because of his greater capacity. Between two persons with equal annual incomes but of whom one owns his house while the other does not, for instance, it would be suggested that the homeowner has the larger tax-paying capacity.

This belief is based largely upon an acceptance of the Crusonia plant view of the permanence of capital. While human beings are viewed as wasting assets, physical capital is viewed as permanent. A person can become ill or injured and will always tire with age. On top of all this, he always lives with the possibility of witnessing a decline in the demand for his services. This view leads to the suggestion that the income from physical capital should be taxed more heavily than the income from human capital, for the higher tax would be designed to compensate for the permanence of the income

---

[13] An "earned" income exemption from the personal income tax could accomplish much the same effect without requiring the development of a new form of tax. The argument that the personal income tax discriminates against human capital is strongest when individuals must pay for their own investment in human capital. Much investment in human capital is subsidized, of course, which reduces the discrimination against human capital. Indeed, it is possible for the amount of subsidy to become large enough even to reverse the direction of discrimination. Consider two initial investments of $100,000, one in human capital and one in physical capital. Suppose the annual gross return is $20,000 in both cases and that annual maintenance costs are $5,000. Let the rate of tax on taxable income be 50 percent. Taxable income from physical capital is $15,000, thus the post-tax rate of return is 7.5 percent. Taxable income on human capital is $20,000, which gives a post-tax return of 5 percent. The impact of "free" education can be illustrated by assuming that the human capital is acquired with a personal outlay of only, say, $50,000. The $5,000 post-tax income from human capital now represents a rate of return to the recipient of 10 percent. Thus the combination of personal income taxation and the heavy subsidization of human capital formation discriminates against physical capital, not human capital.

stream. A progressive tax on wealth, then, becomes viewed as a complement to a progressive tax on income.

In truth, of course, physical capital is not permanent. It, too, can wear out and break down, to say nothing of experiencing a decline in the demand for its services. In this sense physical capital is no different from the human beings who use it. All sources of income will tend to waste away in the absence of conscious economic calculation to the contrary. It is simply erroneous to use the arithmetic of compound interest to portray the inexorability of the income yield from capital.

Nonetheless, an annual net-worth tax, if implemented, would require an annual assessment of such personal assets as real estate, consumer durables, stocks, bonds, bank deposits, and cash. The capricious administration of personal property taxes is widely acknowledged, and it is far easier to value real estate than personal property or intangible assets. Thus an annual net-worth tax would involve several times the administrative difficulties of a personal-property tax. Faced with these realities of tax administration, some analysts have proposed a tax levied upon the estate of a decedent as a convenient substitute for an annual tax on net worth. If wealth accumulation typically begins at age forty and death takes place at seventy, one valuation of wealth upon death would replace thirty during a decedent's life.

Given the amount of tax actually extracted from a decedent's estate, a series of annual taxes could always be designed that would have extracted the same present value.[14] If we assume, for the sake of arithmetic simplicity, that the interest rate is zero, a death tax of $30,000 would be equivalent to an annual series of thirty net-wealth taxes of $1,000 each. Positive interest rates complicate the arithmetic without disturbing the principle of equivalence. The exact impact depends upon whether we take as a base a $30,000 payment upon death or thirty annual payments of $1,000 during life. If equivalence is defined in terms of a $30,000 payment upon death, the annual taxes would be some amount less than $1,000 such that the actual payments plus accumulated interest add to $30,000. If equivalence is defined in terms of thirty annual payments of $1,000, the levy upon

[14] Tibor Barna, "The Burden of Death Duties in Terms of an Annual Tax," *Review of Economic Studies*, vol. 9 (November 1941), pp. 28-39; Nicholas Kaldor, "The Income Burden of Capital Taxes," *Review of Economic Studies*, vol. 9 (Summer 1942), pp. 138-57; A. C. Pigou, *A Study in Public Finance*, 3rd ed. (London: Macmillan and Co., 1942), pp. 138-46.

death would exceed $30,000 by the sum of the accumulated interest earned by the annual payments.

Death taxation may thus serve as a substitute for net-worth taxation, though an imperfect one. An annual net-worth tax would take as its base approximately the entire stock of nonhuman wealth in the economy. But only a small share of the nation's stock of wealth changes hands through death. The total value of gross estates, for instance, each year runs in the vicinity of only about 1 percent of total personal wealth. Consequently, death taxation would serve only imperfectly as a substitute for net-worth taxation.

Saving and the Desire to Bequeath

Economic progress depends heavily upon the rate of saving. The higher the rate of saving, the more rapid the course of economic progress. But how might the taxation of estates or inheritances influence the rate of saving and, hence, economic progress? Before this question can be answered or even addressed, we need some understanding of the forces making for one level of saving rather than another.

A first approximation to the theory of saving suggests that saving is undertaken during working years in order to finance consumption during retirement. This life-cycle theory treats saving as a product of a lifetime plan for earning income and consuming.[15] People are regarded as saving during the earlier years of their lives when their earnings are high in order to finance consumption during the later years when their earnings are relatively low. A well-planned life would be one in which lifetime consumption equalled lifetime income plus the interest earnings on savings.

This perspective seems to account for a considerable amount of saving. It is clearly the case that people save both for unforeseen contingencies and for retirement. But if this were the whole story, people would die penniless, or nearly so. They would not die with much wealth intact; they would not leave bequests behind. The leaving of wealth behind would indicate that the decedent had not

---

[15] Franco Modigliani and Richard Brumberg, "Utility Analysis and the Consumption Function: An Interpretation of Cross-Section Data," in *Post Keynesian Economics*, ed. by Kenneth K. Kurihara (New Brunswick, N.J.: Rutgers University Press, 1954), pp. 388-436; and Franco Modigliani and Albert Ando, "Tests of the Life Cycle Hypothesis of Savings," *Bulletin of the Oxford University Institute of Statistics*, vol. 19 (May 1975), pp. 99-124. For a recent survey, see Alan S. Blinder, "Intergenerational Transfers and Life Cycle Consumption," *American Economic Review*, vol. 66 (May 1976), pp. 87-93.

consumed enough during his lifetime. It would indicate that he had not achieved the proper pattern of saving and consuming over his lifetime. He would be like the long-distance runner who ran a slow pace during most of the race and, finding himself with more energy at the finish then he needed, failed to catch the front-runner.

It could be argued that wealth that was bequeathed rather than consumed was the result of accident or caution. People are notably poor at predicting when they will die. Those who had anticipated living longer than they actually managed to live would quite naturally die leaving some wealth intact. This wealth would be that which they had planned to consume during the remaining years they thought were theirs. On the other hand, those who lived longer than they had anticipated and had allowed for in their life-cycle computations would end up spending their last years as paupers rather than as princes. This latter possibility and the understandable urge to avoid it might dictate a bit of prudence concerning the rate of capital consumption. To the extent that such prudence became dominant, people would generally die leaving part of their estates intact.

This line of argument would suggest that wealth remains unconsumed upon death because our moment of exit is not known to us sufficiently far in advance to allow us to form exactly our life-cycle plan of accumulation and consumption. But the analysis would suggest that if we did know how long we would live, we would consume our final dollar as we exhaled our dying breath. If it were possible to plan one's lifetime pattern of consumption in this way, there would be no reason for wealth to survive the decedent. Toward the end of their lives people would buy annuities, a sort of insurance, to provide them with a stipulated rate of consumption during the remainder of their years. They would transfer title to their wealth and would receive such annuities in exchange. Someone with net wealth of, say, $200,000 at age sixty could exchange his wealth for a guaranteed payment for the remainder of his life. While the length of any particular person's life cannot be predicted, average life expectancy can be predicted quite accurately for a set containing a large number of persons. The relative rarity of such insurance schemes, however, would seem to indicate that the life-cycle framework is not fully descriptive of saving behavior.

It seems clear that some people want to leave bequests for their successors. This bequest motive adds a new dimension to the theory of saving. It is no longer simply a matter of saving during one's working years to finance retirement. Instead, saving is also an expression of peoples' desire to transmit wealth to their successors. The relative strength of these two motives varies, of course, from one person to another. What is important to note, however, is simply that a desire to leave bequests is an important determinant of the amount a person saves. In fact, recent work by Gary Becker suggests that the wealth elasticity of bequests exceeds unity. This implies that a doubling of a person's wealth will more than double his bequests to future generations.[16] This is a very important property of the saving and bequest behavior of testators, as we shall see later. It remains to be seen how the taxation of estates affects saving and, hence, the growth of the capital stock over time.

Estate Taxation and Saving

There are reasons for believing that transfer taxation will impinge especially heavily upon saving, thereby retarding the growth of the capital stock and the pace of economic progress.[17] Transfer taxation, whether of the estate or the inheritance variety, is a tax on one particular manifestation of people's desire to leave bequests for successors, namely, the bequeathing of material wealth. The taxation of material bequests lowers the relative price to decedents of making their transfers of wealth to successors through such nontaxed means as the creation of business, political, and social positions and contacts—and it is a typical human response to shift from taxed to nontaxed activities when one activity becomes taxed while others remain nontaxed. Whether this shift would lead to a reduction in the amount of saving by testators is more difficult to say; as a matter of logical possibility saving might decrease, increase, or remain unchanged, but the weight of evidence suggests that saving would decrease.

We may assume that people who hold wealth upon entering the later years of their lives choose the amount of wealth they want to consume themselves and the amount they want to transfer to heirs. An increase in the rate of estate tax increases the price of providing for one's heirs relative to the price of providing for oneself and relative to the price of providing for heirs in alternative ways. The first law of demand suggests that the quantity of bequests purchased will fall as the price of bequests rises. An increase in tax rates, then,

---

[16] Gary S. Becker, "A Theory of Social Interactions," *Journal of Political Economy*, vol. 82 (December 1974), pp. 1063-94.

[17] See, for instance, C. Lowell Harris, "Revising Estate Taxation," *Tax Review*, vol. 32 (April 1971), pp. 13-16; C. Lowell Harris, "Tax Fundamentals for Economic Progress," *Tax Review*, vol. 36 (April 1975), pp. 13-16; and Dan Throop Smith, "Impact of Federal Estate and Gift Taxes," *Tax Review*, vol. 37 (May 1976), pp. 17-20.

should reduce the volume of bequests made to heirs. But it does not necessarily follow that the tax will diminish saving, that is, encourage dissaving. While less wealth will be bequeathed to heirs, the sum of net bequests and tax payments, which are two alternative uses of savings, might rise, in which case the estate tax will have increased saving.

The impact of estate taxation upon saving will depend upon the testator's elasticity of demand for bequests. There are two elasticities of relevance here, the price elasticity and the wealth or income elasticity. A difficulty arises in that a change in net wealth simultaneously brings about a change in the price of bequests, at least as long as the structure of marginal tax rates is progressive. Similarly, a shift in the rate of tax applicable to any given size of estate will change both the net worth of the testator and the price he must pay per dollar of bequest. The impact of estate taxation upon saving depends on how these two effects of transfer taxation work themselves out. If both effects operate in the same direction, the impact of estate taxation upon saving will be unambiguous. Otherwise, the impact will depend upon the relative strength of opposing magnitudes.

To illustrate the issue, consider a person who is planning his future strategy regarding consumption, saving, and the provision of bequests. Compare his formulation of a plan when he anticipates a zero rate of estate taxation with that when he anticipates a tax rate of 50 percent. With the zero tax rate, $100 (or any multiple thereof) can be transferred to heirs simply by saving $100. This provides a benchmark. To examine the consequences of an increase in the anticipated tax rate to 50 percent of gross estate, we must consider both the wealth effect and the price effect of this change in tax rate.

The anticipation of paying tax will reduce the person's anticipated net wealth. Every dollar he plans to save for bequests will reduce his net wealth by two dollars. As noted above, Gary Becker has argued quite convincingly that the wealth elasticity of bequests will exceed unity.[18] Therefore, a doubling of anticipated net wealth will more than double bequests. Conversely, a halving of net wealth will more than halve bequests. The wealth effect of the increase in estate tax, then, will operate to reduce bequests by more than the increase in taxation. For each $100 that might have been bequeathed under a zero rate of tax, only, say, $40 might be bequeathed under a 50 percent rate of tax, considering only the wealth effect of the tax. And regardless of particular tax rates and amounts of wealth, the

---

[18] Becker, "Theory of Social Interactions."

general principle would be that increases in anticipated tax payments as a result of increases in tax rates would bring about reductions in saving that would exceed the anticipated tax payment. The wealth effect of estate taxation, then, will reduce the total amount of saving.

The increase in the tax rate to 50 percent also increases the price per dollar of bequest to two dollars. To leave a $100 bequest will now require $200 of gross estate, $200 of saving. If the price elasticity of demand for bequests were zero, an increase in taxes would increase savings by the full amount of the tax. As demand becomes more elastic, net bequests will decline. So long as the elasticity of demand is less than unity, however, the total amount spent on making bequests will rise. Less will be transferred to heirs, but the amount transferred to heirs *and* to government will increase. For example, the amount transferred to heirs might be reduced to, say, $60, but to do this would require a gross estate of $120. In this case, the price effect of the estate tax would bring about an increase in saving for the purpose of making bequests.

By contrast, should the demand for bequests be price elastic, the increase in the tax rate will reduce total saving. The tax rise will not just reduce the amount of wealth bequeathed, it will also reduce the amount of wealth expended (and saved) to make the bequest. In this case, the amount of wealth transferred to heirs might be reduced to, say, $40, which would require a gross estate of only $80. If the demand for bequests were price elastic, the price effect would operate to reduce the amount of saving.

The wealth effect of estate taxation will unambiguously reduce the total amount of saving. The price effect, however, will have an ambiguous impact. If the demand for bequests on the part of testators is price inelastic, estate taxation will actually operate to increase total saving. It is only if the demand for bequests is price elastic that the estate tax will reduce total saving. In this latter case, estate taxation operates unambiguously to reduce saving. When demand is price inelastic, however, the effect on savings depends on whether the wealth effect or the substitution effect is larger. There are several reasons for suggesting that the demand for bequests is generally likely to be price elastic, which would indicate that estate taxation would unambiguously reduce saving.

Empirically, Michael Boskin has estimated that the price elasticity of demand for charitable bequests not only is well in excess of unity but also rises along with the price or tax rate.[19] Care obviously

---

[19] Michael J. Boskin, "Estate Taxation and Charitable Bequests," *Journal of Public Economics*, vol. 5 (February 1976), pp. 27-56.

must be taken in inferring from Boskin's results that the demand for bequests in general is price elastic. As discussed in Chapter 4 below, there are plausible grounds for suggesting that the demand for charitable bequests is more elastic than the demand for bequests to personal heirs. Nonetheless, the elasticity of both types of bequests seems likely to be similar. Both types of bequests may be viewed as elements of an overall plan on the part of the testator to save during his lifetime in order to provide for the accomplishment of certain purposes after his death. This makes the two types of bequests complementary elements of the testator's plan for saving and bequeathing, which strengthens the case for assuming that the price elasticity of personal bequests is similar to the price elasticity of charitable bequests.

Furthermore, as a general proposition, the demand for any product becomes increasingly elastic as its price rises. Even the most inelastic of demand functions must become elastic at some sufficiently high price. Otherwise, prices could be increased through taxation until the taxpayer devoted all of his resources to the activity subject to tax. As marginal rates of tax on bequests rise, the demand for bequests will become ever more elastic. This demand may well be elastic even in the lower price ranges, but the elasticity will increase as the price rises, a presumption that corresponds to Boskin's findings. There may possibly be a demand-inelastic region in the lower price ranges, in which event estate taxation will increase total savings undertaken by testators who anticipate paying those lower prices for the bequests they make. But as the price of bequests increases with rising tax rates, the tax will reduce total savings and will do so with increasing force. Because the bulk of estates are transferred by those who face high marginal tax rates, the dominant demands for bequests are likely to be quite elastic. This means that the overall impact of estate taxation will be to reduce the amount of saving, thereby curtailing the rate of economic progress more severely than other forms of taxation.

Plato, Aristotle, and the Transmission of Social Order

Although the taxation of wealth transfers seems clearly to be a practice that reduces levels of saving and future well-being, it receives strong support. Granted, part of this support doubtless comes from the erroneous belief that estate taxation does not influence saving or influences it only slightly. But part of the support for such taxation also seems to reflect a form of social masochism. Many people simply do not like other people to inherit wealth and support transfer taxation to prevent, or at least reduce the incidence of, inherited wealth.[20]

This plea for the socialization of inheritance is reminiscent of Plato's plea for the socialization of parenthood and seems equally unwise. Plato advocated that parents be prevented from knowing which children biologically were theirs. Thus, he thought, all parents would come to feel and act paternally toward all children. Speaking of such communized adults, Plato said that his scheme would

> tend to make them more truly guardians; they will not tear the city in pieces by differing about "mine" and "not mine"; each man dragging any acquisition which he has made into a separate house of his own, where he has a separate wife and children and private pleasures and pains; but all will be affected as far as may be by the same pleasures and pains because they are all of one opinion about what is near and dear to them, and therefore they all tend towards a common end.[21]

Aristotle, with a firmer understanding of human nature, both its possibilities and its limitations, noted in his *Politics* that such a practice would merely result in all parents' acting with equal indifference toward all children. As he put it: "The scheme of Plato means that each citizen will have a thousand sons: they will not be the sons of each citizen individually: and every son will be equally the son of any and every father; and the result will be that every son will be equally neglected by every father."[22] The responsibility of one parent for all children and the absence of particular responsibility for any individual child would produce universal indifference, as Aristotle detected, not universal love, as Plato hoped. An extension of the Platonic idea would support the taxation of bequests, with the ultimate objective being to socialize or to prevent them. Parents would leave wealth not to particular children, but to all children. The

---

[20] Opposition to inheritance on such grounds is developed in Kenneth V. Greene, "Inheritance Unjustified?" *Journal of Law and Economics*, vol. 16 (October 1973), pp. 417-19. Such envy, John Stuart Mill once noted, is "the most anti-social and evil of all passions." "On Liberty," in his *Utilitarianism, Liberty, and Representative Government*, Everyman's Library, No. 482 (London: Dent, 1910, 1859), p. 135. Inheritance is defended in Gordon Tullock, "Inheritance Justified," *Journal of Law and Economics*, vol. 14 (October 1971), pp. 465-74.

[21] "The Republic," in *The Dialogues of Plato*, ed. and trans. by Benjamin Jowett, Vol. I (London: Macmillan, 1892), p. 727.

[22] *The Politics of Aristotle*, ed. and trans. by Ernest Barker (Oxford: Oxford University Press, 1946), p. 44.

Aristotelian perspective suggests the tragic dimension of this policy: the present generation would transmit little wealth to the next.

What are of central interest in this matter are the consequences of different institutions on the character of a social order over time. A primary axiom in this line of inquiry is the partiality of parents for their own children. The Platonic scheme, anti-inheritance, would treat children as common property. Each child would belong to all parents, and each parent would be responsible for all children, that is to say, responsible for none in particular. The taxation of wealth transfers aims to extend this common-property status to material wealth. The Aristotelian scheme, inheritance, would, in effect, treat children as private property. It would play upon and take advantage of the natural partiality of parents toward their own children. The passing on of material wealth is one avenue by which this parental partiality can be expressed.

While economics is noted for the controversy it generates, one of the points of near consensus is that the assignment of common-property status to a resource tends to promote irresponsibility in the use and management of the resource. Aristotle puts this point, like so many others, as well as any modern writer:

> What is common to the greatest number gets the least amount of care. Men pay most attention to what is their own: they care less for what is common; or, at any rate, they care for it only to the extent to which each is individually concerned. Even where there is no other cause for inattention, men are more prone to neglect their duty when they think that another is attending to it: this is exactly what happens in domestic service, where many attendants are sometimes of less assistance than a few.[23]

Or, as he put it even more succinctly: "It is better to be own cousin to a man than to be his son after the Platonic fashion."[24]

To separate one person's possessions from another's is not the social function of a system of private property. This is simply one characteristic of private property. The social function, rather, is to ensure that individual owners husband their resources and put them to good use. In this light, the fencing off of pastures, fishing grounds, and oil deposits are means of ensuring that those resources are used more effectively than they would be used under common ownership. The private-property, free-exchange form of social organization gen-

---

[23] Ibid.
[24] Ibid., p. 45.

erally ensures that one person's more effective use will rebound to the benefit of others.

The parents' natural partiality for their own children is a valuable potential force for good if harnessed by the right institutional framework. This natural partiality is much like someone's natural partiality for his own pasture. There is a social gain to be had from harnessing such natural partialities. As pastures get better attention, all persons, not just pasture owners, gain. So it is with children, even if some receive better attention than others. A Platonic program for ensuring that all children received the same legacy would, if truly implemented, give only a common, low level for all. The prohibition of inheritance and of the sentiments expressed thereby, or even their discouragement through taxation, would facilitate the promotion of a Platonic indifference.

Even if the argument were placed in terms of a conjectural Rawlsian veil of ignorance, it would seem untenable to assert that inheritance would be prohibited or sharply curtailed.[25] It would be just as untenable to assert that the Platonic scheme for child rearing would be chosen. Inheritance, by harnessing the natural partiality of parents for their own children, is an institution that rebounds to the benefit of all. To conduct one's life in such a manner as to leave behind a legacy is commendable and would hardly seem to justify sumptuary taxation. But leaving bequests cannot be encouraged without permitting the existence of recipients; if people are to be encouraged to act as legators, it is necessary that there be legatees.

The opposition to inheritance is based on the assumption that no social function is served by institutions that permit the inheritance of wealth. Yet as the attempt to transfer wealth to heirs comes to be taxed more heavily, saving and the accumulation of wealth will be discouraged. Because transfers of wealth are in large measure expressions of affection or concern of one person for another, the taxation of such transfers would also seem likely to weaken to some extent the underlying affective sentiment that motivates such transfers. It might seem reasonable to discourage activities in which one person takes from another. But why try to discourage those activities in which one person gives to another?

---

[25] The veil of ignorance, which has been used as a conjectural construct on which to base normative assertions, has as its "essential features . . . that no one knows his place in society, his class position or social status, nor does any one know his fortune in the distribution of natural assets and abilities, his intelligence, strength, and the like. I shall even assume that the parties do not know their conceptions of the good or their special psychological propensities." John Rawls, *A Theory of Justice* (Cambridge, Mass.: Harvard University Press, 1971), p. 12.

2
THE EGALITARIAN IMPERATIVE

As a source of revenue, transfer taxation is relatively unimportant. In 1976 transfer taxation accounted for only $5 billion out of total revenues of $300 billion. The primary support for transfer taxation derives from the belief that it is a valuable means of promoting equality in the distribution of wealth. Supporters of transfer taxation believe that the normal outcome of a market economy is increasing inequality in the ownership of wealth and the receipt of income; transfer taxation is seen as a mechanism for offsetting this presumed cumulative process. This chapter explores from several perspectives the egalitarian imperative that has dominated the literature on transfer taxation.

Inequality in Static Perspective

Few topics seem as capable of arousing the passions of intellectuals as the distribution of income and wealth. The basic facts concerning inequality would appear to be quite simple. The lowest fifth of families in terms of income earns just over 5 percent of the income earned by all families, while the second-lowest fifth of families earns just below 12 percent. By contrast, the highest fifth of families earns over 41 percent, while the second-highest fifth earns nearly 24 percent. The distribution of wealth, though documented less extensively than the distribution of income, seems to be even more unequal. It has been estimated that the highest 20 percent of families in terms of wealth own over 70 percent of total net family wealth, while the lowest 20 percent own practically nothing.[1]

---

[1] Lester C. Thurow, *Generating Inequality* (New York: Basic Books, 1975), pp. 3-19.

There are many reasons why figures on the distribution of income and wealth exaggerate the degree of inequality. A proposition that goes back to Adam Smith is that there will be a general tendency in a market economy for income differentials among employments to be such that the net advantages of various employments are equalized.[2] If employments differ in their nonmonetary returns and in the monetary expenses of entering and pursuing them, they will need to differ in their monetary returns as well. Occupations that require long and expensive training before one can earn a livelihood will require higher monetary returns than unskilled occupations just to compensate for the greater cost of entry. Occupations with working conditions that are generally regarded as disagreeable will offer higher returns than occupations in which working conditions are generally regarded as agreeable. In a setting in which people were free to choose among occupations, there would exist an inequality in measured income necessary to offset opposing inequalities with respect to other relevant characteristics.

A few observations on this point seem in order. The relation between age and income is but one factor causing the data to exaggerate the degree of inequality. A lifetime profile of a person's income will typically start low, rise until it peaks during the middle years, then fall off during the retirement years. Suppose all persons have identical income profiles over their lifetimes. If the incomes of persons of different ages are merged to produce a distribution of current income, inequality will appear despite the perfectly equal distribution of lifetime income. This is not to say that all observed income differences are due to such life-cycle considerations, of course, but only that the figures usually ignore such considerations and so exaggerate the amount of inequality.[3]

It is also widely recognized that nonpecuniary differences among occupations cause the statistics on the distribution of income to overstate the extent of inequality. Much of the inequality in the distribution of money income is necessary to offset an opposing inequality in the distribution of nonmonetary forms of income and monetary expenses of earning income. Other things being equal, if people

---

[2] Adam Smith, *Wealth of Nations*, Book I, chap. 10. See also Milton Friedman, *Price Theory* (Chicago: Aldine, 1976), pp. 238-50.

[3] For documentation to the effect that failure to consider the relation between age and income overstates the degree of inequality by about 50 percent, see Mortin Paglin, "The Measurement and Trend of Inequality: A Basic Revision," *American Economic Review*, vol. 65 (September 1975), pp. 598-609. A related analysis is developed in Edgar K. Browning, "The Trend Toward Equality in the Distribution of Net Income," *Southern Economic Journal*, vol. 43 (July 1976), pp. 912-23.

prefer to live in less populous rather than more populous areas at equal wage rates, they will live in more populous areas only if they are compensated by higher wages. Generally, the higher the educational requirements for entering an occupation, the higher the annual income in that occupation. But part of this higher annual income is necessary merely to offset the higher costs of entering that occupation, both the monetary costs of education and the income that could have been earned during the years of schooling. Once again, statistics on the inequality of incomes exaggerate the actual amount of inequality.

Besides considerations of the kind described above, figures on income do not include the in-kind benefits of public spending programs. Edgar Browning has shown that inclusion of such benefits raises the average income of those officially classified as poor in 1973 to 30 percent more than the official poverty level.[4] In 1973, the 23 million people who were officially labeled poor had money income of $20.8 billion, while they would have required $30.5 billion to reach the poverty line. However, they received $18.8 billion in in-kind transfers, which increased their total income to $39.6 billion, 30 percent above the poverty line.

The distribution of wealth is also subject to limitations of measurement that serve to exaggerate the actual degree of inequality. For instance, the standard measures of wealth exclude the wealth implicit in such pension schemes as social security. Yet social security membership can reasonably be conceptualized as a form of wealth. In fact, it is the most important source of wealth for most Americans and totals nearly two-thirds the amount of wealth as commonly defined.[5] An individual has a claim to future benefit payments, and this claim is as much a source of wealth as, for example, endowment insurance policies that might be expected to yield the same payments during retirement. Social security wealth is distributed with considerably more equality than other assets, so the inclusion of this form of wealth would reduce the degree of measured inequality.

Moreover, statistical measures of wealth are measures of the ownership of physical capital only. They exclude any measure of human capital. Yet the human capital that is embodied in people as

---

[4] Edgar K. Browning, *Redistribution and the Welfare System* (Washington, D.C.: American Enterprise Institute, 1975), p. 24.

[5] Martin S. Feldstein, "Social Security, Induced Retirement, and Aggregate Capital Accumulation," *Journal of Political Economy*, vol. 82 (October 1974), pp. 905-26. See also Martin S. Feldstein, "Social Security and Saving: The Extended Life Cycle Theory," *American Economic Review*, Proceedings, vol. 66 (May 1976), pp. 77-86.

a result of education and training increases their income from what it would otherwise have been. The distribution of human capital is considerably more equal than that of physical capital, so inclusion of human capital would also reduce the degree of measured inequality in the distribution of wealth. The exclusion of human capital and social security wealth from common measures of the degree of inequality in the ownership of wealth operates to exaggerate the actual degree of inequality.

Egalitarian Rationalizations

Figures on the inequality of income and wealth, by themselves, provide no basis for judging the performance of an economy. Without some notion of an economically optimal or most preferred degree of inequality, there is no basis for saying whether more or less inequality is preferable to what currently exists. An early and prominent attempt to specify an optimal degree of inequality was Abba Lerner's argument that the optimal degree of inequality is zero.[6] More recently, much literature has carried forward the effort to formulate notions of optimal distributions of income and wealth.[7] This literature generally starts from the proposition that the optimal degree of inequality is zero, assuming that disincentive effects are absent; that is, the proposition holds only if the effort to promote equality does not reduce the total amount of production within the economy. Should the effort to equalize the distribution of income reduce the total amount of production, the optimal amount of inequality would be positive. An analogy to this situation would be cutting larger shares of a shrinking pie. The optimal inequality would occur when a further increase in the share of the pie that is given to those favored by the state leads to a decrease in the absolute amount of pie they receive. This would result because of the reduction in effort on the part of those penalized by the state.[8]

---

[6] Abba P. Lerner, *The Economics of Control* (New York: Macmillan, 1944), pp. 26-32.

[7] See, for instance, Ray C. Fair, "The Optimal Distribution of Income," *Quarterly Journal of Economics*, vol. 85 (November 1971), pp. 551-79; Edmund S. Phelps, "Taxation of Wage Income for Economic Justice," *Quarterly Journal of Economics*, vol. 87 (August 1973), pp. 331-54; and Lester C. Thurow, "The Income Distribution as a Pure Public Good," *Quarterly Journal of Economics*, vol. 85 (May 1971), pp. 327-36.

[8] This point comes across especially clearly in Phelps, "Taxation of Wage Income," p. 334. In his Figure 1, the absence of incentive effects would yield a linear opportunity locus FF, in which case optimality would lie on the 45-degree line, indicating perfect equality.

The canonization of equality has received a big boost from the veil-of-ignorance argument developed by John Rawls—or at least Rawls's construction has been interpreted to this effect.[9] Within the Rawlsian perspective, an optimal distribution of income or wealth is that which would be chosen by the individual members of the society if, at the moment of choice, they thought that they had equally good chances of occupying each position within the distribution of income that might characterize the society. They could be asked to choose, for example, among distributions by quintile in which the shares were, say, 10, 15, 20, 25, 30 in one case and 20, 20, 20, 20, 20 in another. The optimal distribution of income or wealth is simply that distribution that would be chosen by the participants under the conditions postulated. (This theory begs the questions of whether all participants would make the same choice or would even need to make such a choice, to say nothing of whether it is meaningful to speculate about how people with a historic existence would respond if they had no such existence.) In turn, according to Rawls, an optimal set of policies toward the transfer of income and wealth, including transfer taxation, would be that set of policies that would bring the distribution of income and wealth in line with the optimal distribution thus defined.

Optimal Inequality as Holistic Fallacy

The literature on optimal inequality, in assuming that the distribution of income and wealth must be chosen collectively, creates a problem where none exists. At any point in history, of course, there is a single observed distribution of income or wealth among a particular set of persons. It can be described by simple arithmetic. But simple arithmetic can be fallacious economics. This happens when one stumbles from arithmetic to statements such as *"the income distribution is a pure public good. Each individual in society faces the same income distribution."*[10] This argument would hold for practically anything, the distribution of shoes, for instance. At any point in time, each member of society faces the same distribution of shoes. It hardly follows, however, that the shoe distribution must be chosen collectively. And it is no different for the distribution of income and wealth.

In a market economy the distributions of income and wealth,

---

[9] Rawls, *Justice.*
[10] Thurow, "Income Distribution as Public Good," p. 328 (Thurow's italics).

like the distribution of shoes, are products of personal choices by the participants in the economic process. These distributions are the *result* of choices, they are *not* themselves the objects of choice. It is not at all necessary to conceptualize a society as facing a choice among possible distributions, for such a distribution can be simply a product of the choices of the individual members with respect to the conduct of their economic activities.

There are various opportunities for making such choices, and changes in the attitudes generally held by citizens will change the resulting distribution. The choice among occupations is one instance of a choice that affects the distribution of income or wealth. Occupations differ in the distribution of returns they offer; teachers face a far less unequal distribution of returns among themselves than do lawyers. In choosing among occupations a person can take account of his distributional preferences; he can by himself decide whether he wants to take a chance at a large return even though he may fail and end up with a small return. A choice of whether to hire oneself to someone else or to become self-employed is similarly one that allows the individual to exercise preferences on distributional matters.

To say that one must participate in a collective choice over the distribution of rewards is to commit a holistic fallacy. It treats the pattern of distribution as something that must be agreed to and chosen by all for all. But such agreement and choice are unnecessary and would impose uniformity where none is required. The market economy allows persons to make their own choices, and these choices can vary from person to person. Those who want to try for the ecstasy of success even though they risk facing the agony of failure do not need to compromise their desires with those of others who wish to tread a middle road. Observed distributions emerge simply as a product of the choices of the participants in the economy. It is one of the prime virtues of the market form of social organization that such questions as the distribution of income or wealth need never be put to collective choice in the first place.[11]

Redistributive Politics and Egalitarian Excess

While the distributions of income and wealth are the results of personal choices, not an object of collective choice, distributional considerations can influence the character of political outcomes. There

---

[11] This point is developed clearly in Milton Friedman, "Choice, Chance and the Personal Distribution of Income," *Journal of Political Economy*, vol. 61 (August 1953), pp. 277–90.

are strong reasons for suggesting that prevailing political and fiscal institutions will produce an excessive amount of equalization, excessive in terms of the logic used to construct the rationales for egalitarian policies.

Recall the use of the veil-of-ignorance framework for judging various distributive options. The norm within this framework is determined by the hypothetical choices that people would make if they were unaware of their particular position in the distribution of income or wealth. Political outcomes, by contrast, emerge within a context in which people *are* aware of their particular distributional positions. At present, the income or wealth of a majority of citizens is below the average. If these people could truly be placed behind the veil of ignorance, the possibility that they might receive above-average returns would temper their desire for redistribution. However, once they are aware of their distributive positions, they tend to support egalitarian measures. The reverse, of course, holds for that minority of the population with above-average income and wealth. Members of this group would be more willing to support redistribution under the veil of ignorance than if they were aware of their positions in the distributions of income and wealth. This is because, believing that their incomes might be below average, they might expect to gain from redistributive policies. In short, in a world where people are aware of their relative wealth and make choices through political institutions, redistribution will exceed that which would be chosen from behind the veil of ignorance.[12]

Albert Dicey suggested in 1914 that democracy might be unable to withstand the pressures that would be created if the recipients of government transfers were permitted to vote for members of Parliament.[13] Because it is the members of Parliament who choose whether or not to enact the program in the first place, as well as choosing the size of the transfer program, temptations and pressures

[12] See the development of this argument in Richard E. Wagner, "Politics, Bureaucracy, and Budgetary Choice," *Journal of Money, Credit, and Banking,* vol. 6 (August 1974), pp. 370-71. I do not intend to suggest that equalization can be explained wholly by the disparity in the size of above-average and below-average income groups. It surely cannot, for then it would be impossible to explain why full equalization does not result. Rather, the analysis merely suggests than an increase in the size of the below-average group will increase the amount of equalization. For a more complete treatment of equalization within this framework, see Richard E. Wagner, *The Public Economy* (Chicago: Markham, 1973), pp. 168-71.

[13] Albert V. Dicey, *Lectures on the Relation Between Law and Public Opinion in England in the Nineteenth Century,* 2d ed. (London: Macmillan and Co., 1914), p. xxxv.

would be created for the exchange of votes for government subsidies, with the subsidies being paid for by taxes inflicted on other citizens. Dicey expressed this fear in response to a newly enacted pension program in which the recipients, contrary to common practice, were permitted to vote for members of Parliament. Other authors have also expressed concern over the possible political irresponsibility that might arise under progressive income taxation because of the ability of a majority to impose tax rates on a minority that the majority themselves are unwilling to pay.[14] Recent developments in the literature on the political processes through which tax policy emerges do nothing to assuage these fears.[15]

Inequality in Dynamic Perspective

Perhaps the most damaging argument against perfect equality as an ideal, even if we are willing to ignore disincentive effects for purposes of discussion, is that it is an ideal under which few people would want to live. With rare exceptions, people seem to prefer to take a chance at earning an above-average income. One cannot win without taking a chance of losing, and few people play for ties. Individuals will differ in the intensity with which they aspire to win. But, once again, a form of social organization based on a free market is one that gives expression to the whole array of attitudes on this matter.[16]

In gauging the extent to which a social order creates an environment in which its members can lead meaningful lives, the statistical distribution of income may have considerably less importance than the rate of mobility within the distribution, especially among generations. To illustrate, consider three individuals with incomes of $12,000, $8,000, and $4,000. Let us posit that the shape of this distribution will remain unchanged as time passes. One extreme possibility is that a child will come to occupy the same income position as his parents. Thus, children of parents with $12,000 incomes

---

[14] See, for instance, Walter J. Blum and Harry Kalven, Jr., *The Uneasy Case for Progressive Taxation* (Chicago: University of Chicago Press, 1953), pp. 19-21.

[15] Indeed, a considerable amount of inequality is itself a product of legislation. There is a tendency for legislation to produce adverse distributional outcomes, on the one hand, and a proclivity to call for further legislation to promote contrary distributional outcomes on the other hand.

[16] For a discussion of this point and many others in the contemporary literature on material equality, see Leland B. Yeager, "Can a Liberal Be an Equalitarian?" in *Toward Liberty*, ed. by F. A. Hayek, et al. (Menlo Park, Calif.: Institute for Humane Studies, 1971), pp. 422-40.

will themselves earn $12,000, and so forth. The other extreme possibility is that a child's income position will be wholly unrelated to his parents' income position. Thus, children of parents with $12,000 will have an equal chance of earning $12,000, $8,000, or $4,000. In either of these two extreme cases, however, the degree of inequality in the distribution of income will be identical. Yet the two societies would hardly be considered identical. This suggests that the focus of concern ought not to be the amount of inequality in the distribution of income, but the rate of mobility within the income scale. If one-half of the population received $5,000 and one-half received $10,000, the distribution of income would be considerably more equal than the current distribution. Yet this clearly demarcated caste system would probably be rejected by about one-half of the populace.

A substantial amount of mobility seems to exist within the American distribution of income and wealth. In his study of income mobility over time, Lowell Gallaway found that 77 percent of the difference between the average income in the United States in 1960 and the median income of the lowest income class was eradicated within one generation.[17] Table 1 shows that the occupational classification with the lowest income in 1960 was "farm laborers and foremen," which had a median income of $1,066. The median income of sons whose fathers belonged to this occupational class, however, was $4,021. Thus, 77 percent of the gap between their fathers' incomes and the average incomes of all fathers, $4,097, was eliminated by mobility within the income distribution. The opposite effect occurred at the top of the occupational scale. The median income of "managers, officials, and proprietors" in 1960 was $6,640. But the median income of sons from this class was only $5,747. Table 1 shows clearly that sons from the upper income classes tend to earn above-average income while sons from the lower income classes tend to earn below-average incomes. But Table 1 also shows that the income of sons from the upper income classes tends to fall toward the average income while the income of sons from the lower income classes tends to rise toward the average income.

The evidence indicates that individual incomes have a strong tendency to regress toward the mean. While people in the upper income classes are likely to find their relative position worsening

[17] Lowell E. Gallaway, "On the Importance of 'Picking One's Parents'," *Quarterly Review of Economics and Business*, vol. 6 (Summer 1966), pp. 7-15. For a presentation of alternative evidence in support of the same theme, see Christopher Jencks, et al., *Inequality: A Reassessment of the Effect of Family and Schooling in America* (New York: Basic Books, 1972).

Table 1
MEDIAN INCOME OF FATHERS AND SONS,
BY FATHER'S OCCUPATIONAL CLASS,
1960

Father's Occupation	Father's Median Income	Son's Median Income
Managers, officials, and proprietors	$6,664	$5,747
Professional, technical, and kindred	6,619	5,737
Craftsmen, foremen, and kindred	5,240	5,195
Sales	4,937	5,608
Clerical and kindred	4,785	5,504
Operatives and kindred	4,299	4,834
Service, including private household	3,310	4,833
Laborers, except farm and mine	2,948	4,686
Farmers and farm managers	2,169	4,234
Farm laborers and foremen	1,066	4,021

Source: Lowell E. Gallaway, "On the Importance of 'Picking One's Parents',"
Quarterly Review of Economics and Business, vol. 6 (Summer 1966), p. 12.

over time, people in the lower income classes are likely to find their relative income position improving. Children, in other words, are by no means locked into patterns set for them by their parents' place in life. On the contrary, the parents' place seems to exert relatively little influence over the circumstances that come to surround their children. This tendency for income to regress toward the mean seems attributable to two factors. On the one hand, random elements pervade all economic activities, so luck has much to do with one's economic fortunes.[18] On the other hand, biological inheritance, primarily intelligence, places constraints upon the options that one is likely to be able to exploit.[19]

It is well established that intelligence regresses toward the mean. While children of parents with above-average IQs tend to have above-average IQs, their IQs tend to be less than those of their

---

[18] Recall that ancient Hebrew wisdom: "Speed does not win the race nor strength the battle. Bread does not belong to the wise, nor wealth to the intelligent, nor success to the skillful; time and chance govern all." Eccles. 9:11 (*New English Bible*).

[19] James Meade relates differences in income and wealth to differences in luck and inheritance, with inheritance containing four components: genetic, educational, social, and economic. See James E. Meade, *The Inheritance of Inequalities: Some Biological, Demographic, Social, and Economic Factors, Proceedings of the British Academy*, vol. 59 (London: Oxford University Press, 1973).

parents. Table 2 illustrates this regression toward the mean for six occupational classes. While the mean IQ of parents in the higher professional class was 139.7, the mean IQ of their children was only 120.8. And while the mean IQ of parents in the unskilled class was 84.9, the mean IQ of their children was 92.6. From generation to generation, there is mobility within the intelligence scale, even though the inequality in the distribution of intelligence remains constant. Thus, to the extent that high intelligence produces high income, biological inheritance will produce an intergenerational regression toward the mean income.

Luck also plays a strong role in the distribution of income from year to year. Any decision by an entrepreneur to create a new product or by an individual to train himself for a certain occupation is in part a gamble. In all cases an anticipated rate of return may be constructed based on an anticipation of future circumstances. But these anticipations will rarely be realized perfectly. Some people will gain by the discrepancy between anticipation and realization, and some will lose. Some people will have runs of good luck, investing in areas that undergo unforeseeable increases in the relative demands for their output. Others will have runs of bad luck, investing in areas that suffer relative decreases in demand. There is a considerable, largely unappreciated, random variation in the distribution of income, recognition of which casts doubt upon the presumption of cumulative inequality.

Table 2
MEAN IQ OF PARENT AND CHILD,
BY PARENT'S OCCUPATIONAL CLASS

Parent's Occupational Class	Mean IQ	
	Parent	Child
Higher professional	139.7	120.8
Lower professional	130.6	114.7
Clerical	115.9	107.8
Semi-skilled	97.8	98.9
Unskilled	84.9	92.6
Average	100.0	100.0

Source: James E. Meade, *Efficiency, Equality, and the Ownership of Property* (London: Allen & Unwin, 1964), p. 50.

Compound Interest and Cumulative Inequality:
An Erroneous Analogy

Much of the support for transfer taxation has been stimulated by the belief or fear that a market economy tends naturally to produce a cumulative concentration of wealth. The rich are supposed to get richer and the poor poorer. Estate taxation is viewed as a means of offsetting this cumulative process. This belief is based largely on the arithmetic of compound interest and is epitomized by Carl Shoup's statement: "Our existing social values insist upon some limit, or some restraining force, on the accumulation of wealth through gift or inheritance. (*If anyone thinks this is not so, let him keep doubling an amount that he considers acceptable for any one person to control.)*"[20] This line of argument, as fallacious as it is prominent, is worthy of a few observations.

Assertions about the cumulative inequality of wealth are usually derived from a line of argument based upon the arithmetic of compound interest. And the arithmetic of compound interest is truly inexorable. If a capital sum grows at 5 percent compounded annually for thirty years, the terminal value will be 4.32 times the initial value. Under these circumstances, it would take an average rate of tax on estates of 77 percent to prevent the accumulation of wealth from generation to generation. Five percent per year is a very modest rate of return once one allows for inflation. Yet if $1,000 had been invested 200 years ago at 5 percent compounded annually, the present capital value would be $17.3 million. If $1,000 had been invested 200 years ago at 10 percent, which is about the average return on common stock, the present capital value would be $189.7 billion. If wealth actually grew this way, any ten families that had had $1,000 each 200 years ago would together now own practically all of our stock of privately owned wealth.

Although reasoning about wealth based upon compound interest is tempting because of its simplicity, it is contradicted by the evidence. Fortunes do not accumulate at the average rate of return of the economy. Instead, there is a process of growth and decline. Fortunes may grow for a while, but either incompetence or bad luck will ensure their eventual dispersal. The heirs to a fortune are not necessarily as competent as its creator, and even the most competent will eventually come up against bad luck.[21]

---

[20] Shoup, *Federal Estate and Gift Taxes*, p. 108. Italics added.

[21] On these points see George J. Stigler, *The Theory of Price*, 3rd ed. (New York: Macmillan Co., 1966), pp. 307-9.

The unsustainability of wealth holdings is, of course, contrary to the customary argument based on compound interest. The Crusonia plant is the illustration par excellence of compound interest: the more you have the more you get, and that is all there is to it. Life is not so simple once it is recognized that wealth must be consciously and wisely managed to maintain its productive capacity. Wealth is always dissipating, so it must be replaced. It requires the continual application of conscious economic calculation, along with some good fortune, to offset the ever present tendency toward dissipation. According to the compound-interest analogy, the wealthy inexorably become cumulatively wealthier, just as a Crusonia plant becomes cumulatively larger. Obviously, this type of reasoning, even if widely accepted, is inadequate, and some alternative framework is called for.

The problem of "the gambler's ruin" is another model for examining certain facets of the accumulation of wealth over time. In its simplest form, the problem of the gambler's ruin states that the probability that a gambler will lose his fortune varies inversely with the size of his fortune relative to that of his opposition. If the gambler, whose fortune is X, and his opposition, whose fortune is Y, face equal likelihoods of winning, the probability that the gambler will eventually lose his entire fortune is $1-X/(X+Y)$. If the gambler and his opposition are equally rich, 0.5 is the probability of the gambler's eventual ruin.[22]

Especially relevant is the case of the enormously rich adversary. As the wealth of the adversary increases relative to that of the gambler, the probability of the gambler's eventual ruin approaches certainty. In an economic system, an individual striving to accumulate wealth can in certain respects be regarded as similar to a gambler playing against an enormously wealthy adversary. Although acting upon anticipations of such phenomena as demands and technologies is descriptively distinct from playing poker or shooting craps, the uncertainty of outcomes and the repetition of play characterize both settings. These similarities make the analogy helpful as a reasoning device, although the differences between gambling and entrepreneurial activity should also be kept in mind.

Of even greater interest than the probability that any given fortune will be exhausted is the expected length of time it will take to exhaust the fortune. It is relatively uninteresting by itself to argue

---

[22] The problem of the gambler's ruin is surveyed in William Feller, *An Introduction to Probability Theory and its Applications*, vol. 1, 2d ed. (New York: John Wiley and Sons, Inc., 1957), pp. 311-13.

that any fortune will eventually disperse, for the process might take 50 years or 500. The expected length of time it will take for the gambler to become ruined can be quite important: it makes a difference whether the expected duration is 50 years or 500.

The entries in Table 3 show the probability of ruin in a two-person game and the expected duration of play for several values of p, q, X, and Y. The general outlines of the table are unmistakably clear.[23] Even when he has a 0.5 chance of winning, the gambler's chance of ruin is 0.9 when he has 10 percent of the total wealth and rises to 0.99 when his share of the wealth falls to 1 percent. When the probability of the gambler's winning falls below 0.5, his eventual ruin is practically certain, even when he initially possesses 10 percent of the wealth. The expected duration of play is highly sensitive to the probability that the gambler will win. When the gambler initially has 10 percent of the wealth, the expected duration of play before ruin is 900 trials. The expected duration falls to 50 when the probability of winning falls to 0.4 and falls to 30 when the probability of success falls to 0.33.

We can now examine the role that confiscatory rates of taxation play in the process of the accumulation and dissipation of wealth over time. An entrepreneur makes investments in alternatives whose future payoffs are uncertain. Sometimes he will win; sometimes he will lose. Other things being equal, the more progressive the rate of tax on winnings, the less willing an entrepreneur will be to take risks. The greater the rate of progressivity, the higher the excess tax on gains vis-à-vis losses. Under a proportional income tax, for instance, an income of $100,000 one year and zero the next will pay the same tax as annual incomes of $50,000 for two years. Under progressive taxation, however, the tax on $100,000 will be more than twice as large as the tax on $50,000.

Whereas an individual might be willing to make an investment with a probability of success of only, say, 0.40 under proportional taxation, he might require a probability of success of 0.45 under

---

[23] Let p denote the probability that the gambler wins and q the possibility that he loses. If $P = q$, the probability that the gambler will become ruined is:

$$P_r = 1 - X/(X + Y). \text{ If } p \neq q, P_r = \frac{(q/p)^{(X + Y)} - (q/p)^X}{(q/p)^{(X + Y)} - 1}.$$

If $p = q$, the expected duration before ruin will be:

$$D_r = XY. \text{ If } p \neq q, D_r = \frac{X}{q - p} - \frac{X + Y}{q - p} \cdot \frac{1 - (q/p)^X}{1 - (q/p)^{(X + Y)}}.$$

Table 3

PROBABILITY OF GAMBLER'S RUIN AND EXPECTED DURATION OF PLAY

Initial Fortunes of		Probability of		Probability of Gambler's Ruin (P_r)	Number of Plays Expected Until Ruin (D_r)
Gambler (X)	Opposition (Y)	Gambler's winning (p)	Gambler's losing (q)		
10	90	0.5	0.5	0.9	900
10	90	0.4	0.6	1.0 [a]	50 [a]
10	90	0.33	0.67	1.0 [a]	39 [a]
10	990	0.5	0.5	0.99	9900
10	990	0.4	0.6	1.0 [a]	50 [a]
10	990	0.33	0.67	1.0 [a]	30 [a]

[a] These values are extremely close approximations. The exact entry for P_r in the second row is 0.999999. Similarly, the exact value for D_r in the second row is 49.999999.

Source: Author's computations. For formulae, see text p. 35 and footnote 23.

progressive taxation. And the higher the rate of tax on winnings, the more favorable the odds must be before an entrepreneur will make the investment. And the more favorable the odds, the slower the expected disintegration of the entrepreneur's fortune. The use of progressive rates of tax to penalize those with high income and large wealth will tend to promote a conservatism that reduces the rate of personal mobility within the distributions of income and wealth.

In the absence of inflation, government bonds would be a riskless investment. And if investments were truly riskless, the arithmetic of compound interest would exert itself. The higher the rate of tax on the accumulation of wealth, the more numerous will be the number of people who settle for lower, more certain returns. Fortunes are much less likely to erode under such circumstances. And the fortunes that do erode will erode at slower rates. On the one hand, high tax rates will encourage safe investments, which reduce the probability of ruin and lengthen the duration of time before ruin. On the other hand, by reducing the rate of mobility among wealth positions, high rates of tax also reduce the ability of newcomers to enter the high-wealth brackets. On both grounds, then, high rates of tax promote the retention of large amounts of wealth by those who already possess them.[24]

The progressive taxation of incomes and estates produces results that are clearly inconsistent with the desire to make it possible for all individuals to have reasonable opportunities to become wealthy. Present policies protect holders of previously accumulated wealth, both from themselves and from the competition of others who might otherwise amass new wealth. Some penalty is placed upon existing wealth holders, but a more severe obstacle is thrown in the path of those who are not wealthy but who might be inclined to attempt to become wealthy. In consequence, there is a tendency for wealth to beget wealth in a manner that would not take place if efforts to penalize high incomes and wealth through taxation were relaxed.

---

[24] It is noteworthy that, in the postwar period of confiscatory taxation, capital gains have been the primary route by which new private wealth has been amassed. Earnings taken in this form, of course, are subject to lower tax rates. Rather than being looked upon as a loophole, however, the capital gains provision should be looked upon as a second-best provision in our tax system, with considerably lower tax rates being first best.

3

CAPITAL APPRECIATION UNREALIZED AT DEATH

The tax treatment of capital appreciation has created much controversy, and this controversy raises issues that relate both to income taxation and to estate taxation. Before the Tax Reform Act of 1976, any capital gains that were unrealized at the time of death escaped liability for income tax.[1] Unrealized appreciation was not included in the decedent's final income-tax return, and the successor was able to adopt the market value of the assets at the time of the decedent's death as his cost basis for calculating future capital gains. Unrealized capital appreciation amounts to more than one-third of the gross value of estates, and its ability to escape taxation was widely described as one of the major failings of our system of income taxation.[2] In its 1969 proposals for reform, the Treasury Department recommended that unrealized capital gains on assets transferred upon death be subject to ordinary capital-gains taxation as part of the decedent's final income-tax return.[3] The 1976 act did not adopt this recommendation but instead provided that the decedent's original basis would be carried forward to his heirs. This chapter explores the tax treatment of unrealized capital appreciation, although it necessarily touches upon the tax treatment of realized capital appreciation as well.[4]

---

[1] For an estimation that full taxation of unrealized capital gains would have increased tax revenues in 1967 by $1.9 billion, see Peter Eilbott, "The Revenue Gain from Taxation of Decedent's Unrealized Capital Gains," *National Tax Journal*, vol. 22 (December 1969), pp. 506-15.

[2] See, for instance, Jerome Kurtz and Stanley S. Surrey, "Reform of Death and Gift Taxes: The 1969 Treasury Proposals, the Criticisms, and a Rebuttal," *Columbia Law Review*, vol. 70 (December 1970), pp. 1365-1401.

[3] U.S. Treasury Department, *Tax Reform Studies and Proposals*, Part I (Washington, D.C.: 1969), pp. 28-29.

[4] For a survey of some of the pertinent issues, see Harold M. Somers, "Taxation of Capital Gains at Death," in *Public Finance and Welfare*, Paul L. Kleinsorge, ed. (Eugene: University of Oregon Press, 1966), pp. 135-55.

Unrealized Appreciation before the Tax Reform Act of 1976

Before the Tax Reform Act of 1976, estates were accorded different tax treatment depending on the extent to which capital appreciation was realized or unrealized. Realized capital appreciation was and still is treated as income during the year in which the appreciation is realized: one-half of the appreciation is entered as income in computing liability for income tax for that year. Whether the appreciation represents an increase in the real value of the asset or whether it merely reflects the inflation of prices is irrelevant. The tax treatment is the same in either case. The tax treatment of realized capital appreciation, it should be noted, is strictly a problem of income taxation. The issues it raises are those surrounding the definition of income within a system of income taxation. No issues pertaining to estate taxation are involved.

Unrealized capital appreciation, by contrast, raises issues relating both to income taxation and to estate taxation. Prior to the 1976 act, unrealized capital appreciation was not subject to income taxation, though the appreciation entered into the base of the estate tax. If the appreciation had been realized before death, it would have been subject to income tax; held until death, however, the unrealized appreciation was not subject to income tax. In either case, the estate tax was assessed against the market value of assets in the decedent's estate. Contention arose because less tax was paid on the devolution of an estate that included unrealized capital appreciation than on that of an estate in which capital appreciation had been realized before death; the tax paid on realized appreciation was not paid on unrealized appreciation. This differential tax treatment was reinforced by the ability of the successor to value the assets at their current market value in forming his basis from which any subsequent capital gains would be computed. In this manner, unrealized appreciation completely escaped liability for income tax.

Unrealized Appreciation Since 1976

This ability of capital gains transferred upon death to escape income taxation inspired numerous suggestions for revision. The Treasury Department, in its 1969 proposals for tax revision, suggested that such capital gains be included in the decedent's final income-tax return. This proposal, known as constructive realization, was supported on the grounds that it would make the taxation of unrealized appreciation consistent with the taxation of realized appreciation. This would be accomplished by treating a taxpayer upon death as if he had realized all capital gains before death—that is, by including such gains in the decedent's final income-tax return.

In place of constructive realization, the 1976 act provided that unrealized capital gains should continue to be ignored for tax purposes, but that the donor's basis would be carried forward to the donee. Thus, realized and unrealized appreciation receive similar tax treatment under the present law. In this case, however, the focus is not on the owner of the asset, but on the asset itself. That is, tax liability depends on the sale of the asset, not on the death of the owner. The principle that gains are taxed only when realized is maintained, only now all capital realization will carry a liability for income tax.

Some simple arithmetic can illustrate the differences among the three approaches. Suppose assets initially purchased for $100,000 are valued at $300,000 at the time of the owner's death. Under the rules prevailing before the 1976 act, the $200,000 of capital appreciation would not be taxed in the decedent's final income-tax return. The heir, moreover, would have been able to enter $300,000 as his basis value for the asset. Should the value of the asset subsequently rise to $500,000 and then be sold, the realized capital gains would be $200,000. Under the 1969 proposal for constructive realization, a capital gain of $200,000 would have been declared in the decedent's final income-tax return. A second gain of $200,000 would have been declared in the heir's income-tax return when he sold the asset for $500,000. Under the provisions of the 1976 act, no capital gains would be declared at the time of the owner's death. The heir's basis, however, would remain at $100,000. The subsequent sale for $500,000, therefore, would produce a capital gain of $400,000 to be declared in the heir's income-tax return. This last is the procedure now in force.

It was often argued that the pre-1976 tax treatment of unrealized capital appreciation created a "lock-in" effect. The idea was that some investments were maintained in their present form rather than being liquidated and placed in new form because the act of liquidation would call forth a tax liability that could be postponed if the old pattern of investment were continued. The new investment opportunities might well offer a higher return gross of tax. But to switch investments would require the investor to realize the gain on his former investment. Once the tax that would be assessed on this realization were taken into account, it might prove rational to retain the former investment pattern. This lock-in effect, to the extent that it exists, is a result of the progressive rate structure of our personal income tax. Because of this progressivity, the potential tax liability increases with disproportionate rapidity as unrealized capital gains increase. So the larger the capital gains, the stronger will be the lock-in effect due to the rising relative tax burden.[5] The carrying forward of the original basis adopted in the 1976 act, it is clear, will tighten this lock-in effect. Because the capital gains, which are taxed according to a progressive rate structure, will tend to be larger when they are realized by the heirs than if they had been realized a generation earlier, tax considerations will come to weigh more heavily in decisions whether to realize capital gains in order to switch investments.

Capital and Income

The reason for the 1976 revision in the tax treatment of unrealized appreciation was the inconsistency in the tax treatment of realized and unrealized appreciation. Although the act is now law, it is worth noting that this inconsistency could have been removed in one of two ways. The first, that actually adopted, is the requirement that the old basis be carried forward to the new owner, which brings the tax treatment of unrealized appreciation into line with that of realized appreciation. Unrealized capital appreciation now carries a potential tax liability that can no longer be erased by death.

It would also have been possible to bring the tax treatment of realized appreciation into line with that of unrealized appreciation. If one person is taxed more heavily than another when it is judged that the two should be taxed equally, there are two ways of achieving equal treatment. One is to raise the tax on the person less heavily burdened. It is also possible, however, to lower the tax on the person more heavily burdened. The existence of two alternative avenues for removing the inconsistency in tax treatment warrants further examination, for their respective merits depend on some fundamental principles regarding the meaning of capital and income.

Is capital appreciation appropriately defined as income? If so, it is an appropriate object of taxation under a system of income taxation. The suggestion that unrealized appreciation should be taxed upon death in the decedent's final income-tax return is based upon

---

[5] For a sample of this literature, see Gerard M. Brannon, *The Lock-in Problem for Capital Gains: An Analysis of the 1970-71 Experience* (Washington: Fund for Public Policy Research, 1974); Martin David, *Alternative Approaches to Capital Gains Taxation* (Washington, D.C.: Brookings Institution, 1968); and Henry C. Wallich, "Taxation of Capital Gains in the Light of Recent Developments," *National Tax Journal*, vol. 18 (June 1965), pp. 133-50.

the presumption that such appreciation is properly classified as income. But if capital appreciation is not appropriately defined as income, the tax treatment of unrealized capital appreciation becomes the standard for the taxation of realized capital appreciation as well.

The Haig-Simons definition of income has been used to rationalize the taxation of capital appreciation.[6] Income, in this case, is defined as the sum of annual consumption and all changes in net worth over the year. Capital appreciation, even if unrealized, is clearly income within this definition, for it increases net worth. While it is usually recognized that the annual taxation of capital appreciation is the ideal under this definition, it is also usually acknowledged that the delay of taxation until the asset is sold is an expedient alternative. Taxation upon realization is generally regarded as a reasonable and workable compromise.

The Haig-Simons definition of income, however, is not the only possible definition. Moreover, it is generally regarded as severely flawed. Its most glaring conceptual weakness is that it confounds terribly the important distinction between capital and income, between the stock value of an asset and the flow value of the output emanating from that asset.

While many authors have attempted to develop definitions that distinguish between capital and income, the most generally accepted approach has been that of Irving Fisher.[7] An economy may be characterized at any time as containing a stock of productive assets, and these assets will be capable of yielding some sustainable flow of output. The value of the stock of assets is the value of capital, and capital appreciation refers to increases in the value of this stock of assets. The value placed on the flow of output from that stock of assets is income. This distinction between capital and income does not, it might be noted, imply acceptance of the Crusonia plant metaphor, for the potential output is not automatic and permanent; it will not be realized and maintained in the absence of continual and appropriate economic calculation and decision making. Rather, it suggests that the stock of productive assets and the rate of output that potentially can be produced by that stock of assets are two distinct magnitudes.

---

[6] A statement and defense of this concept of income is contained in Henry C. Simons, *Personal Income Taxation* (Chicago: University of Chicago Press, 1938).

[7] Irving Fisher, *The Theory of Interest* (New York: Macmillan, 1930). For a recent discussion of the confounding of capital and income, which is epitomized in proposals to tax capital appreciation as income, see Dan T. Smith, "Capital Gains, Losses in Income Taxation," *Tax Review*, vol. 33 (December 1972), pp. 45-48.

Capital Appreciation in a System of Income Taxation

The operation of these alternative approaches to capital appreciation in a system of income taxation may be illustrated quite simply. Under the Haig-Simons definition, income is equal to consumption plus changes in net worth. Income is, in other words, the maximum amount of consumption that could be undertaken without reducing the capital value of assets. Consider a person who owns an apple orchard containing 1,000 trees, with each tree yielding, on average, 500 apples annually. This orchard will run the gamut from newly planted trees to fully mature trees, with each year the oldest trees being replaced by new trees. It so happens that the steady-state, sustainable yield of this orchard is 500,000 apples annually. Suppose the annual yield of 500,000 apples yields a net income of $50,000 annually, deductions having been made for expenses of production and of replacing aged trees. While each apple has a net value of ten cents, each tree would have a net value also. Suppose each tree would have a net value of $50, reflecting a 10 percent rate of interest. Under these circumstances, the income from the orchard is $50,000 annually and the capital value of the orchard is $500,000.

Now suppose that, in response to the rising cost of medical services, people began eating an apple a day. As a result of this rise in demand for apples, the price of apples rises. Let us assume that the price doubles. The 500,000 apples produced annually by the orchard would now bring in a net income of $100,000. The doubling of the value of the orchard's yield would, in turn, increase the value of the orchard itself. It is reasonable to assume that the value of the orchard would rise to $1 million, for there is no reason to assume any change in the rate of time preference and the interest rate. Under the Haig-Simons definition of income, the owner of the orchard would have had an income of $600,000 in the year in which the price of apples doubled. Of this amount, $100,000 would represent the net income from the sale of apples, and $500,000 would represent the appreciation in the value of the orchard itself.

The conceptually superior Fisherian definition of income brings a quite different perspective to the matter. One must begin by asking: Why has the value of the orchard increased to $1 million? The answer, of course, is that it has increased *because* the price of apples and, thereby, the income from the orchard have risen. The rise in capital value, in other words, is merely a reflection of the increased income yielded by the orchard. A failure to tax the capital appreciation is *not* a defect or loophole in a system of *income* taxation. On the contrary, such nontaxation of capital appreciation is necessary for the very integrity of a system of income taxation. The capital gain of $500,000 should not be taxed simply because it is not income. The rise in capital value is reflected in the larger income flow, and in a system of income taxation it is the income flow that should be subject to tax. The $500,000 increase in capital value is simply incidental to the $50,000 increase in annual net income. The capital gain is nothing but the capitalization of the increased income flow.

To tax both the income flow at its larger rate and the gain in capital value is to engage in a double counting that totally confounds the fundamental distinction between a flow of services and the stocks of assets that produce those services. The capital appreciation is merely the reflection, the present value, of the enlarged income flow which is already being taxed. Taxation of the income flow at, say, 20 percent annually would be equivalent to taxation of the capital value at 2 percent annually, under the postulated conditions of a 10 percent rate of interest. Simultaneous taxation of the income flow and the capital value would, of course, double the rate of taxation; in other words, it would represent double taxation. In this regard, not only the expansion in the income-tax coverage of unrealized appreciation that occurred in the 1976 act should be reversed, but also the other instances of taxing capital appreciation within our system of income taxation should be curtailed.[8]

---

[8] Admittedly, this statement regarding the nontaxation of capital gains is something that would be tempered by certain pragmatic considerations, for pragmatic implementation is not as simple as the conceptual illustration may suggest. Capital assets will not necessarily generate corresponding income flows. The tax treatment of owner-occupied housing serves as a good example. The flow of services from such housing is not taxed as income, while capital gains on sales of residences are taxed, though many countries do tax the imputed income of owner-occupied housing. Similarly, common stocks may yield no dividends, while appreciating in value nonetheless. In either of these two cases, as well as in many others, annual measures of income may not correspond closely with income interpreted as a sustainable flow of services from an asset. In many respects, the replacement of our system of personal income taxation with one of consumption taxation might have much to commend it, for consumption is a more accurate indicator of permanent income on the one hand, and such a shift would avoid such problems as that illustrated by the appreciation of common stock on the other hand. These possibilities, however, are beyond the scope of this volume.

45

4
TRANSFER TAXATION AND CHARITABLE BEQUESTS[1]

Bequests to a variety of philanthropic institutions are currently deductible from the gross estate in determining a decedent's taxable estate. The deductibility of charitable bequests has inspired intense controversy, as critics of deductibility have claimed that the charitable deduction should be regarded as a governmental subsidy for the charitable activities of the wealthy. The issues arising from the charitable deduction and our various policy options in this matter will be examined in this chapter. The impact of alternative rates of estate taxation upon the volume of charitable bequests will also be examined.

The Charitable Deduction and Tax Expenditure Rhetoric

It is commonly argued by its opponents that the charitable deduction is a form of government subsidy, a "tax expenditure." The deductibility of charitable bequests means that the amount of tax levied on an estate is reduced as charitable bequests are increased. This point is easily illustrated. Suppose initially that there is no deductibility of charitable bequests and that a taxable estate of $1 million is taxed at an average rate of 50 percent.[2] The state claims $500,000. Suppose

---

[1] Much of the material in the first three sections of this chapter is based upon a paper I prepared for the Commission on Private Philanthropy and Public Needs. For the original, more complete treatment, see Richard E. Wagner, "Death, Taxes, and Charitable Bequests," in Commission on Private Philanthropy and Public Needs, *Compendium of Research Papers* (Washington, D.C.: U.S. Treasury Department, forthcoming).
[2] The actual tax burden under the post-1976 rate structure, and in the absence of gifts, would be $345,000, but the various arithmetic examples used here are based on round numbers as a matter of convenience.

that $300,000 of the remainder goes for private bequests and $200,000 goes for charitable bequests. Compare this setting with one in which charitable bequests are fully deductible from the decedent's gross estate. Since the taxable estate falls to $800,000, the tax burden placed on the estate falls to $400,000. If charitable bequests remain at $200,000, the amount of wealth transferred to private persons will increase to $400,000. In this case, the making of a $200,000 charitable bequest reduces the amount remaining for heirs by only $100,000, for the other $100,000 is in effect financed by a reduction in tax collections.

In the more general case, part of the $100,000 reduction in tax liability would accrue to charitable organizations rather than to private persons. This consideration, however, does not alter the central point that bequests to charitable organizations are financed in part by reductions in tax collections by government. With a marginal tax rate of 50 percent, the introduction of deductibility means that each $100 of charitable bequests results in a $50 reduction in the government's tax take.

Through the use of such arithmetical analogies, it is often suggested that the charitable deduction should be viewed as a government subsidy, a "tax expenditure," in contrast to a direct expenditure of public revenue. If the deductibility of charitable bequests were eliminated, the additional tax revenue that would accrue to the public treasury could be used to finance some program of direct public expenditure. The deductibility of charitable bequests, it is suggested, can be viewed as enabling individual testators to make decisions concerning the expenditure of public revenue. In the absence of deductibility, tax collections would have been higher, so additional public expenditure could have been undertaken. Thus interpreted, the charitable deduction diverts government revenue from categories of expenditure that would have been chosen collectively to categories of expenditure that are chosen privately.

Moreover, if the charitable deduction is viewed as a government subsidy, it is a subsidy whose amount would appear to rise directly with the tax rate, and, hence, the wealth of the testator. Indeed, the commotion that has been raised about the charitable deduction revolves not so much around the fact of subsidization as around the argument that the deduction allows some testators to transfer wealth to their preferred recipients on more favorable terms than other testators. Compare two testators, one in the 30 percent marginal-rate bracket and the other in the 70 percent rate bracket. For each dollar transferred to exempt institutions by the testator in the 30 percent rate bracket, his tax liability is reduced by thirty cents. This means that the personal net cost of the one dollar transfer is seventy cents. By contrast, the transferor in the 70 percent rate bracket is able to secure a seventy cent reduction in tax liability for each dollar transferred. In this case the personal cost of the one-dollar transfer is thirty cents. In terms of remaining net estate, each dollar of transfer costs the less wealthy testator more than twice what it costs the more wealthy testator. The charitable deduction, it is suggested, not only allows private testators to direct the expenditure of what may be regarded as public revenue but also allows relatively wealthy testators to exert disproportionately large influence over the use of such diverted revenue. It is this type of reasoning that has led to a variety of proposals for substitute means of supporting private philanthropy.[3]

Suggested Policy Alternatives

Those who feel that the charitable deduction is a form of government subsidy have suggested a variety of alternative policies. One option, of course, is simply to eliminate the deductibility of charitable bequests. The best estimate of the consequences of such a policy change is that it would bring about at least a 50 percent reduction in the volume of charitable bequests.[4] Other options that would not curtail charitable bequests so sharply have also been advocated. One option would simply place a ceiling on the charitable deduction. A second option would substitute some form of tax credit for the charitable deduction. Still a third option would replace the charitable deduction with a program of governmental grants to charitable institutions.

A ceiling on deductibility. It is sometimes suggested that the deductibility of charitable bequests be retained, but that a ceiling be placed on the amount that can be deducted.[5] Fifty percent is the figure that has been bandied about most often. With such a ceiling, charitable bequests would still be deductible in determining taxable estate, but only so long as they did not exceed 50 percent of the

---

[3] Many of these proposals are described in the work of the Commission on Private Philanthropy and Public Needs. See its report, *Giving in America* (Washington, D.C.: Commission on Private Philanthropy and Public Needs, 1975), as well as the various relevant technical documents cited in the appendix to the report.

[4] Michael J. Boskin, "Estate Taxation and Charitable Bequests," *Journal of Public Economics*, vol. 5 (February 1976), pp. 27-56.

[5] Such ceilings are applied in the income-tax treatment of charitable contributions.

gross estate. Bequests in excess of this ceiling would not be deductible under this option. Any such ceiling, by increasing the price to testators of making charitable bequests, would reduce the amount of such bequests. And the lower the ceiling, the greater the reduction in charitable bequests. A 50 percent ceiling, it is estimated by Boskin, would generate nearly a 10 percent reduction in charitable bequests.[6] Moreover, the estimated $189 million reduction in charitable bequests would be offset by only a $43 billion increase in tax revenues.

Support for ceilings rests primarily upon the belief that no estate should escape tax liability altogether, even if the testator should bequeath his entire estate to charity. This sentiment is analogous to that which supports the principle of a minimum income tax—the belief that no person should escape liability for income tax, even if his income were zero under the prevailing definition of income. To acknowledge that an analogy exists is not, of course, to provide a rationale for such sentiments, which seem to be more appropriately consigned to the realm of irrational passion than to that of rational thought.

A related option that has been suggested on occasion is that a percentage limitation on the charitable deduction be applied only to bequests to private foundations as distinct from bequests to public charities. Alternatively, limitations could be applied to both types of bequest, with a lower limit for bequests to private foundations. Any such use of differential limits on the charitable deduction will promote a shift in the composition of philanthropic activity away from private foundations and toward public charities.[7] This proposal reflects a misguided belief that the social value per dollar of wealth flowing to public charities exceeds the social value per dollar of wealth flowing to private foundations. Its advocates also express the concern that foundations are sometimes used by testators as devices to enable heirs to maintain control over their wealth without having to pay estate tax. An examination of this issue would raise considerations of how to assess the performance of what might be called the "philanthropic industry" and lies beyond the scope of this volume.[8]

A tax credit for charitable bequests. A tax credit has also re-

---

[6] Boskin, "Estate Taxation."

[7] The personal income tax currently imposes such a differential limitation, the ceiling being 20 percent on contributions to private foundations and 50 percent on contributions to public charities.

[8] For a brief consideration of some aspects of this topic, see Richard E. Wagner, "Tax Policy Toward Private Foundations: Confused Principles and Unfortunate Legislation," *Policy Studies Journal*, vol. 5 (Spring 1977), pp. 314-19.

ceived considerable attention as a substitute for deductibility. The rate of credit could be either fixed or variable and could be set at any of numerous rates or rate structures. A fixed rate of credit would reduce estate tax liability by the product of the rate of credit and the amount of charitable bequest. With a 30 percent rate of credit, for instance, estate tax liability would fall by $30 for each $100 of charitable bequest. With a variable rate of credit, by contrast, the marginal rate of credit would vary with changes in, for example, the taxable wealth of the testator or the relative share of charitable bequests in the testator's gross estate.

A fixed rate of credit would be considerably less complex than a variable rate of credit because it establishes a constant price for charitable bequests, regardless of the wealth of the testator. This price is equal to one minus the rate of credit. A 30 percent rate of credit, for instance, yields a price of seventy cents per dollar of charitable bequests. Any such credit whose rate lay between the lowest and the highest marginal rates under the present rate schedule would discourage charitable bequests by those in the upper wealth brackets and would encourage charitable bequests by those in the lower wealth brackets. A rate of 30 percent is the marginal tax rate applicable to the $100,000 to $150,000 taxable-estate rate bracket. Hence, a 30 percent credit would discourage charitable bequests by those with more than $150,000 of taxable estate, while encouraging charitable bequests by those with taxable estates of under $100,000. Moreover, a 30 percent credit, Boskin estimates, would generate nearly a 20 percent reduction in the total volume of charitable bequests.[9] In addition, the resulting $360 million in charitable bequests would be offset by only $227 million of increased tax collections.

There exists, of course, some rate of credit that would leave the total volume of charitable bequests unchanged, though the relative importance of different testators in directing wealth to various charitable activities would change. The required rate of credit would be somewhat larger than the 30 percent rate analyzed by Boskin. Suppose, for purposes of discussion only, that the break-even rate is 41 percent, which is the marginal tax rate applicable to taxable estates in the $1–$1.25 million bracket. Assuming that charitable bequests would be unchanged if the charitable deduction were replaced by a 41 percent credit, testators with estates below $1 million would increase their charitable bequests, while testators with estates above $1.25 million would reduce their charitable bequests.

---

[9] Boskin, "Estate Taxation."

A matching grant to charitable organizations. It has also been suggested that the charitable deduction could be replaced by a program of matching grants to philanthropic institutions.[10] In principle, such a program of matching grants could be designed to achieve any desired volume of support for philanthropic institutions. Although the proposal for a matching-grant system has received support as if it were substantially different from a tax-credit system, there is essentially no difference between a tax credit and a matching grant. A 30 percent credit means that tax liability is reduced by $30 per $100 of bequest, which, in turn, means that a $70 bequest by the testator is, in effect, matched by $30 from the government. A 30 percent credit is identical to a 43 percent matching grant. Under the 43 percent matching grant, a $70 charitable bequest would be matched by a $30 payment from the Treasury, presumably to the philanthropic institution designated by the testator.

There seem to be only two differences of any importance between a tax credit and a matching grant. First, the matching grant would be administratively wasteful in comparison to the tax credit. To generate the same amount of charitable bequests under the matching grant, the government would need to determine the amount of bequests received by each charitable recipient, to compute the amount of matching funds to be received by each recipient, and to prepare and send the checks. None of this effort would be required under a program of tax credits. Second, one of the historical lessons of the revenue-sharing program is that controls will always be placed on revenues that are spent through grant programs, and, moreover, demands will be expressed at various points in the political system for the strengthening of such controls.

In Support of the Charitable Deduction

The concern over the properties of alternative policy options for replacing the charitable deduction is predicated upon the belief that the charitable deduction is appropriately regarded as a government subsidy. There are strong grounds, however, for suggesting that the charitable deduction should not be viewed as a government subsidy.[11]

---

[10] See, for instance, Paul R. McDaniel, "An Alternative to the Federal Income Tax Deduction in Support of Private Philanthropy," in *Tax Impacts on Philanthropy* (Princeton: Tax Institute of America, 1972), pp. 171-209.

[11] See, for instance, William D. Andrews, "Personal Deductions in an Ideal Income Tax," *Harvard Law Review*, vol. 86 (December 1972), pp. 309-85; and Boris I. Bittker, "The Propriety and Vitality of a Federal Income Tax Deduction for Private Philanthropy," in *Tax Impacts on Philanthropy*, pp. 145-70.

The point of contention is easily illustrated. Consider three testators, A, B, and C. Let A and B each possess an estate of $1 million and let C possess an estate of $500,000. Assume that A transfers his estate wholly to surviving members of the family, while B transfers $500,000 to surviving members and $500,000 to charitable institutions. Assume that C transfers his estate wholly to surviving members. The controversy over the charitable deduction, when viewed in this context, is whether B should be treated as an equal of A or as an equal of C. The view that the charitable deduction should be treated as a government subsidy implies that B should be treated as equal to A. The view that the charitable deduction should not be treated as a government subsidy, but rather as a fully appropriate practice, implies that B should be treated as equal to C. The issue, then, can be reduced to one of choosing just who is to be treated as B's equal for purposes of taxation.

The point of dispute is the distinction between charitable and noncharitable bequests. The thought patterns of many economists lead them to treat charitable bequests and contributions as ordinary acts of consumption. This perspective underlies the literature on utility interdependence, for instance, and the popularity of this literature would seem to suggest that the conceptualization of charity as an act of personal consumption is consistent with the views of many economists.[12] In making a choice of whether, and to whom, to make a charitable contribution or bequest, a donor must, by definition, choose his preferred alternative. In this literature, a donor is viewed as choosing how to allocate his income or wealth between purchases for his own consumption and purchases for the consumption of others, an allocation problem that is indistinguishable from the ordinary one of allocating one's budget among ordinary commodities. The "price" of charitable contributions is, quite simply, the amount of personal consumption that is forgone by virtue of making the contribution. An individual will expand his contribution to others as long as the marginal rate of substitution of contributions for his own consumption exceeds the ratio of the price of contributions to the price of his own consumption.

Consider two testators, D and E, each of whom bequeaths $500,000 to finance various vacation activities. In D's case, the bequest finances the purchase of a sumptuous summer home for members of the family. In E's case, the $500,000 is used to finance a program of

---

[12] See, for instance, Harold M. Hochman and James D. Rodgers, "Pareto Optimal Redistribution," *American Economic Review*, vol. 59 (September 1969), pp. 542-57.

summer vacation camps for inner-city youth. In both cases, according to the perspective that treats charitable bequests as consumption by the donor, the testator is giving up $500,000 and is receiving a "service" in exchange. It merely happens that in one case this service is a vacation for one's progeny, while in the other case it is vacations for strangers. Both patterns of bequest, then, would be regarded as instances of ordinary self-indulgence, with the only difference between the two being the object of indulgence.[13]

This perspective seems to obscure almost totally the distinction between self-indulgence and self-denial. A different perspective would suggest that the deductibility of charitable bequests and contributions is fully appropriate as a matter of principle and is necessary for arriving at a definition of taxable income or wealth. It seems clear that there is an economic aspect to all action, but this is not to say that all action is economic or even that the economic motive is dominant in all action. Economic action, in this contrasting framework, is characterized by *non-tuism*. As Philip Wicksteed described it, non-tuism is present whenever one party to an exchange is not swayed by the opposing interest of the other party.[14] It means not that there are discernible instances of pure, self-interested action which can be called "economic" but only that there are instances in which the seller does not modify his selling price simply because of the buyer's desire for a lower price. Wicksteed gave the illustration of Paul making tents in Corinth. Paul's primary interest was to support his evangelical work, not to increase his wealth or consumption. Yet, so long as Paul, in selling his tents, did not allow himself to be influenced by the desires of purchasers for lower prices, the transaction between Paul and his customers was non-tuistic, or purely economic. Only if Paul had allowed himself to be influenced by his customers' desires for lower prices would tuistic elements have emerged, in which case the transaction would have ceased to be purely economic.

Charitable contributions and bequests seem generally to be dominated by tuistic sentiments. It is precisely the taking into account of the interest of the *other person* that characterizes the charitable act. The physician who donates his services one day per week to a charity clinic is in the position Paul would have been in had he

---

[13] As Boris Bittker notes, this frame of analysis "requires gifts to charities to be classed with wine, women, and song." Boris I. Bittker, "Charitable Contributions: Tax Deductions or Matching Grants?" *Tax Law Review*, vol. 28 (Fall 1972), p. 47.
[14] See Philip H. Wicksteed, *The Common Sense of Political Economy* (London: Macmillan, 1925), pp. 173-77 for a characterization of economic behavior in terms of the predominance of non-tuistic sentiments.

allowed himself to be swayed by his customers' desires for lower prices. The situation is the same with the testator whose bequest finances a summer vacation camp for inner-city youth. Granted, there may be economic considerations involved in selecting among subjects for contributions or bequests, but the economic aspect is of a distinctly secondary order of importance. For the most part, however, our customs, laws, and institutions treat charitable activity as being outside the realm of profit-seeking activity, for tuistic sentiments dominate the former activity, but not the latter.[15]

When viewed from this perspective, two testators with equal wealth should not be subject to equal amounts of tax if one makes more charitable bequests than the other. Rather, the person whose charitable bequests are larger should be regarded as having less wealth than the other person and accordingly should pay less tax. Therefore, it would seem necessary to deduct charitable bequests in computing taxable estate. The aforementioned $500,000 bequest to finance summer vacations for inner-city youth should be viewed not as an act of consumption by the testator, an act of self-indulgence, but rather as analogous to a cost of acquiring income or disposing of an estate, an act of self-denial. Therefore, the present tax treatment of charitable bequests, in which such bequests are fully deductible, would seem to be entirely appropriate as a matter of principle.

The argument that the charitable deduction subsidizes especially the philanthropic activities of the wealthy would seem to be erroneous, once it is recognized that non-tuistic sentiments dominate charitable activity. Consider the previous illustration of three testators, A, B, and C. It is true that the charitable bequest reduces the tax liability of B by more than it would reduce the tax liability of C, should C make the same size bequest. This effect, however, is due simply to the arithmetical consequences of progressive rates of tax and cannot be regarded as a subsidization of testator B. When the deductibility of charitable bequests is viewed as appropriate as a matter of principle, the empirical evidence regarding the impact of deductibility on charitable bequests is seen somewhat differently.[16] It is no longer

---

[15] This point is developed forcefully in Bittker, "The Propriety and Vitality of a Federal Income Tax Deduction for Private Philanthropy." A related argument, although not developed in the context of the deductibility of charitable bequests, is William Breit, "Income Redistribution and Efficiency Norms," in *Redistribution Through Public Choice*, ed. by Harold M. Hochman and George E. Peterson (New York: Columbia University Press, 1974), pp. 3-21.

[16] Recall that Boskin estimated that the deductibility of charitable bequests induces the wealthy to make about twice the charitable bequests that they would have made in the absence of deductibility.

a matter of using this evidence in order to construct a case for deductibility. The case for deductibility exists independently of the empirical evidence, whatever it may happen to show. Rather, deductibility is an institution that induces the wealthy to divert an even larger portion of their wealth than they would otherwise into uses that are beneficial to others.[17]

Estate Taxation and Support for Philanthropic Institutions

While the charitable deduction has come under strong attack in recent years, it is a practice that is firmly based on principle. Its defense need not rest on judgments about its empirical impact in stimulating charitable bequests. The strong empirical impact that deductibility seems to provide is just frosting on the cake, so to speak. While deductibility stimulates charitable bequests, it should be noted that this does not mean that charitable bequests are higher under estate taxation combined with deductibility than they would be if estate taxation were curtailed or abolished. Indeed, there is good reason for believing the contrary.

Because estate taxation depresses savings and capital accumulation, reduction or elimination of the tax would increase these magnitudes. While this decline in tax burden would increase the price of charitable bequests relative to personal bequests, it would also provide more wealth for bequests of both types. Therefore, the impact of estate taxation on charitable bequests depends on the relative strength of these two opposing effects. To the extent that the wealth effect dominates the relative price effect, the estate tax depresses the volume of charitable bequests, the mitigating effect of deductibility notwithstanding.

It seems reasonable that most testators will place first priority on providing for their families rather than for institutions, and this presumption is supported by empirical evidence. Loosely speaking, this presumption means that the family will be taken care of first and philanthropic institutions will share with government what remains of the estate. The available evidence clearly supports this presumption about testator choice. The Treasury's special tabulations of estate tax returns for 1957 and 1959 show that charitable bequests were less than 4 percent of gross estates of less than $900,000, while nonchari-

---

[17] C. M. Lindsay, "Two Theories of Tax Deductibility," *National Tax Journal*, vol. 25 (March 1972), pp. 43-52, develops two reasons for deductibility, the second of which conforms to this interpretation of the charitable-bequest deduction.

table bequests were about 76 percent and taxes about 20 percent. Among estates exceeding $10 million, however, charitable bequests were about 30 percent and noncharitable bequests and taxes about 35 percent each.[18]

As the average size of estates rises, bequests to institutions increase relative to bequests to persons. Such evidence as this suggests that testators tend to look after their families first, with institutions receiving second consideration. While the demand for bequests seems likely to be price elastic on the whole, the demand for personal bequests seems to be less elastic than the demand for philanthropic bequests. Under these circumstances, an increase in estate taxation will reduce the total volume of bequests, but it will reduce the volume of charitable bequests more than that of personal bequests. Conversely, a reduction in estate taxation not only would increase the total volume of bequests but also would increase charitable bequests more than it would increase personal bequests.

A simple numerical example might be useful to illustrate the point. Consider a person who plans to leave a target level of wealth to his family, giving the remainder to charitable institutions. Suppose that this target level of giving to family members is $300,000 and further suppose that he would leave a gross estate of $1 million if the rate of tax were 33 percent. This 33 percent tax rate means that it would cost $150,000 to leave $300,000 for the family, in which event $550,000 would remain for charity. If the rate of tax were 50 percent, the cost of leaving $300,000 for the family would be $300,000, in which event only $400,000 would remain for charity, assuming that the total estate remained at $1 million. The higher tax rate would, of course, bring about a reduction in the total size of the estate, which would reduce still further the amount of the charitable bequest. Conversely, an elimination of the tax would increase the amount of charitable bequest to $700,000. And this does not take into account the additional increase in charitable bequests that would result from the increase in the size of the estate due to the lowered tax rate.

An assumption of a target level of bequests to family members is, of course, an assumption of zero elasticity of demand and is made here only to simplify the arithmetical illustration. In the more general case of less than complete inelasticity, a rise in the tax rate from 33 percent to 50 percent would reduce the amount transferred to the family to some amount less than $300,000. Yet the amount of

---

[18] Robert Anthoine, "Testamentary Trusts," in *Federal Estate and Gift Taxes* (Washington, D.C.: The Brookings Institution, 1966), p. 155.

bequest plus the concomitant tax liability would still exceed $450,000, which would still leave less than $550,000 for charitable bequests, again assuming, for computational simplicity, that the increased tax rate did not reduce the total estate. Taking account of the impact of the tax in reducing the total size of the estate would indicate an even larger decline in the amount transferred as charitable bequests.

Estate taxation, therefore, impinges especially heavily upon the supply of wealth to philanthropic institutions. Yet private philanthropy serves a valuable function in our social order in supporting a variety of exceedingly important activities whose support otherwise would depend upon the bestowal of political favor. Private schools and universities provide alternatives to government in educating the populace. Religious institutions provide an important diversity in the articulation of cultural norms and common concerns, as well as in the undertaking of certain charitable activities. Private foundations offer alternative sources of support for a variety of scientific, cultural, and charitable activities. By diminishing contributions to private philanthropic institutions, estate taxation promotes government monopoly over such areas. Yet concern for the maintenance of basic liberties, the preservation of minority preferences and points of view, and effectiveness in providing services all suggest that competition among institutions providing related services is preferable to monopoly.[19] Tax institutions that erode support for private philanthropy should not be greeted warmly.

---

[19] See William A. Niskanen, *Bureaucracy and Representative Government* (Chicago: Aldine, 1971) for a discussion of many facets of these issues of competition and monopoly.

5

INFLATION, PROGRESSIVITY, AND REAL RATES OF TAX

The federal estate tax was enacted in 1916 and, with the exception of a change in the marital deduction in 1948, remained unchanged between 1942 and 1976. During this latter period, consumer prices increased by 275 percent. Between 1916 and 1976, moreover, consumer prices increased by 425 percent. When a tax system has a progressive rate structure, as our estate tax and our income tax do, inflation leads to an increase in real tax burdens even though there has been no change in the nominal rate and bracket structure. This chapter considers how inflation has this impact and then describes the effect of inflation on the specific exemption and on the rate and bracket structure. The arithmetical illustrations that follow are based on the structure of the tax as it existed before the Tax Reform Act of 1976. This is done because the central point can be presented more clearly in a context in which the essential structure of the tax remains unchanged than in a context in which this structure changes. Furthermore, nothing in the post-1976 tax structure negates any of the arguments developed below about the impact of inflation.

A General Perspective

When a tax is a fixed proportion of the tax base, an inflationary increase in the tax base has no impact on the real rate of tax extracted from citizens. An inflationary doubling of all taxable incomes will, in a system of proportional income taxation, double the nominal amount of everyone's income tax liability. Because both income and tax liability have exactly doubled, disposable income has doubled also. This means that the real rate of tax has not changed. The same would be true with a proportional rate of estate taxation. With a tax rate of 10 percent, a $50,000 estate will be taxed $5,000, assuming no exemptions for the sake of arithmetical simplicity. In the face of 100 percent inflation, the value of the estate would become $100,000 and would carry a tax liability of $10,000. The net estate with inflation, $90,000, is equal in real value to the net estate without inflation, $45,000. In real terms, the inflation would have no impact on the real burden of the estate tax.

The invariance of real tax burdens in the face of inflation vanishes under progressive taxation. Inflation now has the effect of increasing the real burden of taxation. With progressive taxation, the average rate of tax rises with the tax base. While inflation increases the tax base, it increases tax burdens even more rapidly.[1] Under 1976 rates, for instance, a taxable estate of $250,000 would have carried a tax liability of $65,000. Should inflation have boosted the taxable estate to $500,000, the tax liability would have risen to $145,700. Taxes would have risen from 26 percent of the estate to over 29 percent, even though the real value of the estate would have remained the same. Put differently, the post-inflation disposable estate of $354,300 would be worth only $177,150 in pre-inflation dollars. This is a decline of 4 percent in real value, due to nothing more than the tax-increasing effects of inflation in a tax system with a progressive rate structure. In higher wealth ranges, where the tax rates are higher, the tax bite of inflation is even sharper. The inflationary doubling of a $2.5 million estate to $5 million would have destroyed 16 percent of the real value of the disposable estate. And the inflationary doubling of a $5 million estate to $10 million would have destroyed 23 percent of the real value of the disposable estate.[2]

Actually, it does not really matter whether the increase in income or wealth results from inflation or from economic progress. With economic progress, just as with inflation, progressive taxation will ensure that real rates of tax automatically will increase. A doubling

---

[1] For an examination of this point with reference to income taxation, see James M. Buchanan, "Inflation, Progression, and Politics," in *Inflation, Economic Growth, and Taxation*, Proceedings of the 29th Session (1973) of the International Institute of Public Finance (Barcelona: Ediciones Alba, S.A., 1975), pp. 45-66; James M. Buchanan and James Dean, "Inflation and Real Rates of Income Tax," *Proceedings of the National Tax Association* (1974) (Columbus, Ohio: National Tax Association, 1975), pp. 343-50; and Alan P. Murray, "Income Tax Progression and Inflation," *Tax Review*, vol. 35 (December 1974), pp. 47-50.

[2] Dan Throop Smith argues that the best way to assess the effect of inflation in increasing real tax burdens is to consider its impact in reducing disposable income, not to consider its impact in increasing tax liability. See his "Progressive Income Taxation Discriminates Against Larger Incomes During Inflation," *Tax Review*, vol. 36 (June 1975), pp. 23-28.

of wealth or income will still generate a greater than doubling of tax extractions.[3] In the pure inflationary setting, the rising real rate of tax reduces real disposable wealth or income. When the growing real tax burden is the result of progressive taxation operating within a regime of economic progress, real disposable wealth or income still manages to rise, but it rises more slowly than tax liability.

The resort by governments to inflationary finance generates two sources of tax revenue for government. The first hinges on the fact that inflation is a tax on money balances. The creation of new money by government reduces the real value of the nominal money balances held by private citizens. For instance, a printing of money by government that doubled the stock of nominal money balances would, as a first approximation, destroy one-half of the real value of the nominal money balances held by private citizens.[4]

The other source of tax revenue from inflation is the increase in the real rates of such taxes as the estate tax and the personal income tax. That is, we are taxed once by inflation and once again through the effect of inflation in increasing the real burdens of other taxes. It is important to note that this piggyback increase of taxes occurs automatically. There is no deliberation over whether or not to impose a tax surcharge. Inflation enacts such a surcharge without any need for legislative action—so the publicity that any such action on the part of Congress would bring never materializes. These automatic tax increases receive little if any notice; they are brought to public attention much less forcibly than are explicit proposals for higher taxes. Yet in consequence, the size of the public sector becomes larger than it would otherwise have been. Wallace Oates's finding that government spending grows more rapidly, under inflationary conditions, as the tax structure becomes more progressive corroborates this proposition.[5]

Indexation has sometimes been suggested as a way of correcting for this upward bias in tax rates in an inflationary environment. The central idea behind indexation is to make changes in real tax liability

---

[3] For a discussion along with some suggestions for correction, see John O. Blackburn, "Implicit Tax Reductions with Growth, Progressive Taxes, Constant Progressivity, and a Fixed Public Share," *American Economic Review*, vol. 57 (March 1967), pp. 163-69.

[4] Milton Friedman, "Government Revenue from Inflation," *Journal of Political Economy*, vol. 79 (August 1971), pp. 846-56.

[5] Wallace E. Oates, " 'Automatic' Increases in Tax Revenue—The Effect on the Size of the Public Budget," in *Financing the New Federalism*, Wallace E. Oates, ed. (Baltimore: Johns Hopkins University Press, 1975), pp. 139-60.

responsive only to changes in real magnitudes. This objective would be achieved by indexing both the basic exemption and the rate and bracket structure. A tax with a basic exemption of $10,000 would have that exemption increased to $20,000 in the face of a doubling of the selected price index. A rate and bracket structure that ran from zero to $10,000, $10,000 to $50,000, and $50,000 and up would be revised to run from zero to $20,000, $20,000 to $100,000, and $100,000 and up in response to the doubling of prices. Indexation, with all the debate that has emerged over it, is distinct from, though related to, the problems discussed in this volume and cannot be examined here. Nonetheless, any consideration of the impact of inflation upon real rates of tax necessarily brings to mind indexation as a possible policy option.[6]

Illustrations

The federal estate tax initially became effective on September 9, 1916. At that time, the range of coverage was small and the progression in tax rates was slight. After a specific exemption of $50,000, the marginal tax rates ranged from 1 percent on the first $50,000 of taxable estate to 10 percent on taxable estates in excess of $5 million. While the specific exemption was $60,000 in 1976, the real value of this exemption in 1916 dollars would have been less than $15,000, a mere 30 percent of its initially chosen real value. Put differently, the specific exemption in 1976 would have had to exceed $200,000 merely to equal the real value of the $50,000 exemption in 1916. The $60,000 exemption dates from 1942. This amount of exemption in 1976 would have been equivalent in real terms to an exemption of just over $20,000 in 1942 dollars, little more than one-third of its initial real value. To restore the real value of the specific exemption to its 1942 level would have required an exemption of nearly $180,000 in 1976.

The 1976 act increased the exemption to $175,625.[7] When viewed in light of the impact of inflation in increasing real tax burdens, this increase in the level of exemption would approximately compensate

---

[6] Different perspectives toward indexation are presented in Herbert Giersch et al., *Essays on Inflation and Indexation* (Washington, D.C.: American Enterprise Institute, 1974). See also Geoffrey Brennan, "Inflation, Taxation, and Indexation," *Policy Studies Journal*, vol. 5 (Spring 1977), pp. 326-32.

[7] Actually, a credit of $47,000 replaced the specific exemption, but an exemption of $175,625 is equivalent in value to this credit.

for the inflationary erosion of the real value of the exemption since 1942, but that is all. Yet this increase in the exemption is generally treated by proponents and opponents alike as a proposal for *tax reduction*—demonstrating how people are unconscious of the tax increases that occur automatically through inflation.

The current rate and bracket structure was instituted in 1941. The constancy of this rate and bracket structure despite nearly four-fold inflation has also served to increase real rates of tax. Some comparisons of the current rate and bracket structure with those that applied in 1916 and 1941 are instructive.

Between 1916 and 1976, the minimum rate of tax increased from 1 to 3 percent, and the size of the estate subject to the minimum rate of tax shrank from $50,000 to $5,000. To allow for inflation, however, the lowest rate bracket in 1976 would have to begin at over $200,000 to provide coverage comparable to that of 1916. On top of this inflationary erosion in the real size of the minimum rate bracket, the actual rate of tax was also increased by 300 percent. The highest rate bracket in 1961 began at $5 million; in 1976, an upper bracket of over $20 million would have been required to offset the inflation. Moreover, the rate of tax applicable to this highest bracket was increased by 770 percent. Estates that were valued at less than $3 million in 1916 would have been valued at more than $12 million in 1976, even though their real value was unchanged. With reference to the 1976 rate structure, the $12 million taxable estate would carry a tax liability of $7,628,200, leaving a net estate of only $4,371,800. If this rate structure were indexed with reference to 1916, the tax on this $12 million estate would have been $5,052,800. The disposable estate would have been $6,947,200. This is nearly 60 percent higher than the real value in the absence of indexing. In this case, the impact of inflation in moving an estate of unchanged real value into higher nominal-rate brackets would have destroyed nearly 40 percent of the real value of the net estate.

A comparison with 1941 presents a similar picture, though the inflation has been less and the rate and bracket structure has remained unchanged. A taxable estate of $5,000 would have been taxed $150 in 1941. This very same estate would be valued at nearly $15,000 in 1976, so would be taxed $1,110. The remaining disposable estate of $13,890 would in real 1941 terms be worth only about $4,630. The increase in the real tax rate due to inflation would have reduced the real size of the disposable estate by nearly 5 percent.

A taxable estate of $1 million in 1941 would have borne a tax of $325,700, which would have left a net estate of $674,300. This very same estate in 1976 would have been valued at nearly $3 million. Such an estate would have carried a tax liability of $1,263,200, leaving a net estate of $1,736,800. Furthermore, inflation would have shrunk the real value of the net estate to $578,900. In this instance, inflation would have destroyed 14 percent of the real value of the estate.

The effect of inflation is strongest in the higher brackets, for both estate and income taxes. Take the highest bracket. In 1941, $10 million of taxable estate would have carried a tax liability of $6,088,200, leaving $3,911,800. This very same estate in 1976 would have been valued at nearly $30 million, an amount that would have been taxed $21,488,200. When converted to real terms, the remaining estate of $8,511,800 would have been worth only $2,837,300. In this instance, the inflationary increase in real rates of tax would have destroyed more than 27 percent of the real value of the estate.

Another way of presenting the impact of inflation on real rates of tax is to compare the rate and bracket structure in 1976 with that which existed in 1942. If the inflation that has taken place in consequence of the government's printing of money to finance part of its activities could be offset through indexation, what would become of the currently existing tax structure? To offset the impact of the inflation, to have equal real values bear equal real tax burdens despite the impact of inflation on nominal values, all of the rate brackets would have to be three times larger in 1976 than in 1942. The 3 percent rate applicable in 1976 to the $0–$5,000 bracket would become applicable to taxable estates in the $0–$15,000 range. Similarly, the $5,000–$10,000 bracket, the second lowest, would increase to $15,000–$30,000. Similar adjustments would have to take place throughout the rate and bracket structure. The $250,000–$500,000 bracket would become a $750,000–$1.5 million bracket. The $2–$2.5 million bracket would become a $6–$7.5 million bracket. The highest marginal rate, 77 percent, would apply only to taxable estates in excess of $30 million. And the total tax on an estate of $30 million would be $18,264,600, whereas actually it is $21,488,200. Inflation, in other words, reduced the net value of such estates by nearly 30 percent.

The inflationary activities of the state, it is patently clear, have widened enormously the applicability of the estate tax and have increased substantially the amounts extracted by that tax. The progressive nature of the new rate and bracket structure will make possible the same tax-increasing impact of inflation in the future. These tax increases occurred, and will continue to occur, silently.

6
TECHNICAL ISSUES CONCERNING TRANSFER TAXATION

The preceding three chapters have examined three sets of issues regarding our system of transfer taxation. This chapter is a potpourri of four remaining issues.

The Marital Deduction and the Unit of Taxation

When one spouse dies before the other, should a tax be levied upon the estate of the first to die? Present practice is to levy a tax, although there is a marital deduction of the larger of $250,000 or one-half of the decedent's adjusted gross estate. The Treasury's 1969 proposals, on the other hand, advocated that no tax be levied under these circumstances; that is, that a 100 percent marital deduction be implemented. One's choice of the appropriate unit upon which to base tax liability depends primarily upon one's attitude toward the attribution of ownership. In some legal frameworks, property is vested in the family unit rather than in the separate members of the family. Under such circumstances there can be no institution of inheritance, since the surviving members of the family unit cannot inherit what already belongs in common to the family unit.[1] Our legal framework recognizes and assigns individual ownership of property, so a decedent's property devolves upon someone else through succession—an institution that came into being only as societies came to recognize individual rather than family ownership of property.[2]

The federal estate tax recognizes individual rather than family

---

[1] See, for instance, William Shultz's description of the Hindu joint-family system in which there is no inheritance because property is owned in common by the family and is acquired by survivorship rather than by succession. William J. Shultz, *The Taxation of Inheritance* (Boston: Houghton-Mifflin, 1926), p. 33.

[2] Eugene F. Scoles and Edward C. Halbach, Jr., *Problems and Materials on Decedent's Estates and Trusts* (Boston: Little, Brown and Co., 1965), p. 5.

ownership of property, though the 50 percent marital deduction represents a partial recognition of family ownership. Prior to the Revenue Act of 1942, deaths occurring in community-property states were taxed less heavily than deaths occurring in common-law states. In community-property states, property acquired after marriage by one spouse is attributed equally to both spouses, while in common-law states all such property is attributed to the spouse who acquires the property. If the estate tax were a proportional tax, the same tax burden would arise in either state. But under a progressive rate structure, the total tax liability on a given amount of wealth becomes ever larger the more unequally it is distributed. This property of progressivity would result in higher estate taxation in common-law states than in community-property states.

The Revenue Act of 1942 eliminated this differential tax treatment. It did so by treating deaths in community-property states as if they occurred in common-law states. The tax liability of decedents in community-property states was increased to the same level as that borne by decedents in common-law states. The Revenue Act of 1948 maintained the equality of treatment, only it reversed the standard for comparison. Deaths occurring in common-law states were now treated as if they occurred in community-property states. This statutory change lowered the tax liability of decedents in common-law states to the level borne by decedents in community-property states. This was done by allowing a 50 percent marital deduction on non-community property. The Tax Reform Act of 1976 kept the 50 percent marital deduction, but added the option of a flat $250,000 deduction.

Even with the 50 percent marital deduction, two families of identical wealth can bear different tax liabilities depending upon whether the richer or the poorer spouse dies first. No universal rule in this matter can be stated, however, because the outcome depends on the actions of the surviving spouse in conserving or in dissipating the estate, as well as on the time that elapses between the deaths of the two spouses. The time elapsing between the two deaths is important because of the provisions for quick succession relief: If the second spouse dies within two years of the first, the second estate is given credit for 100 percent of the tax payment on the estate of the first spouse. If the second death occurs within three or four years of the first, the rate of credit is lowered to 80 percent. This credit is lowered in 20 percent increments for each two years that elapse between the deaths, until the credit vanishes once the second spouse has survived the first by ten years.

66

Consider the case of a noncommunity-property state in which the husband's wealth is $1 million and the wife's is zero. If the husband predeceases the wife, the marital deduction can be taken by the wife. This would reduce the husband's taxable estate to $500,000, ignoring for computational ease such complexities as those due to the unified credit and to possible charitable bequests. The wife's subsequent taxable estate would, as noted above, depend on her disposal of the estate and on how long she survived her husband. Assume that she conserves the estate intact, consuming only the interest. If she survives her husband by less than two years, her taxable estate will be $500,000. If she survives her husband by ten years or more, her taxable estate will be $844,200. The total taxable estate will be the sum of the separate taxable estates of the husband and the wife. This figure will range from $1 million to $1,344,200.

Should the wife predecease the husband, no marital deduction could be taken. When the husband died, the taxable estate would be $1 million. In this instance, the total estate tax would be $345,800. By contrast, the total tax paid on two estates of $500,000 each would be $311,600. At the same time, the total tax payments on two estates of $500,000 and of $844,200 respectively would be $435,438. These computations suggest considerable variability in tax liability, depending both on the order of death and on the time that elapses between the two deaths.

At a zero rate of interest, this type of comparison would be all there was to the matter. With a positive rate of interest, however, the comparison is not so simple. A dollar paid today is more onerous than a dollar that must be paid, say, two years from now. When tax payments differ in their timing, it is the present values of those payments, not the actual amounts, that must be compared. Consider the case in which the two spouses die within two years of each other, say one year and 364 days apart. If the richer spouse dies first, a tax payment of $155,800 is made at that time and another payment of $155,800 is made two years later. If the poorer spouse dies first, a single payment of $345,800 is made in two years. Which order of death carries the higher tax liability in present value terms? Obviously, this depends on the rate of discount. If the rate of discount is 10 percent, the two present values are relatively close. The single payment in two years carries a present value of $285,785. The two payments spread two years apart carry a present value of $284,560. At a 10 percent rate of discount, then, the tax burden is heavier if the poorer spouse dies first. And this would become even more so as the rate of discount fell below 10 percent. But with higher rates of discount, the positions would be reversed; the higher tax liability would occur if the richer spouse died first.[3] It is clear that the order of death can affect the amount of tax liability of families with equal wealth. Which order of death is less heavily taxed, however, will itself depend upon and vary with the rate of discount.

While the Treasury's 1969 proposals for transfer tax reform supported an unlimited marital deduction, the 1976 act maintained the 50 percent limit, though it also provided for a minimum deduction equal to the total amount transferred to the surviving spouse up to a limit of $250,000. The central rationale for an unlimited marital deduction is the belief that it is unreasonable to treat the surviving members of a family as receiving a capital gain when one member dies. Quite the contrary. The death of either the husband or the wife leaves the remaining members of the family worse off. There are obvious material dimensions to this. If the family includes children at home, the death of the mother will sharply increase the cost of maintaining the family because many of the services typically provided free by the mother must now be purchased. The death of the father will also sharply reduce the income available to support the family. And then there is the nonmaterial loss, which mocks any suggestion that the family has become wealthier.

Because the family is usually considered the basic unit of ownership de facto, even though not de jure, the surviving members of the family do not acquire additional physical capital by virtue of the death of one member. Furthermore, the family has suffered a reduction in the stock of human capital available to it. If the family were treated as the unit of taxation, a tax would be levied as property devolved from the family unit. No tax liability would result from the death of one member of the family so long as there was a surviving member.[4] Such a change would bring the unit upon which tax liability is based into line with prevailing attitudes about the appropriate unit of ownership of property. It would seem that a transfer tax should be levied, if one is to be levied at all, only if there is a clear capital gain to the recipient, and this would seem to require adoption of the family as the unit of taxation.

---

[3] At a 20 percent rate of discount, for instance, the present value of the two payments spread two years apart is $263,994. By contrast, the present value of the single payment delayed two years is only $240,139.

[4] For an early treatment of succession defined in terms of the family unit, see Harold M. Groves and Wallace I. Edwards, "A New Model for an Integrated Transfer Tax," *National Tax Journal*, vol. 4 (December 1953), pp. 353-60.

Liquidity Problems of Closely Held Businesses

The liquidation of assets to pay estate tax can create special difficulties when the assets are not readily marketable. This is often true with closely held businesses and family farms. Considerable evidence suggests that the need to liquidate the assets of closely held businesses to pay estate tax encourages mergers of such businesses with larger corporations. Chelcie Bosland, for instance, estimates that in 63 percent of mergers of closely owned businesses over the period 1955–1959, estate-tax considerations played a significant factor in the decision to merge.[5] Two separate motivations seem to lie behind the desire to merge closely owned businesses. On the one hand, there is a fear that the estate will not have sufficient liquidity to pay the tax, and the merger is a source of liquidity. On the other hand, the amount of tax liability to be assessed is itself uncertain because it depends upon an arbitrary valuation of the business by the Internal Revenue Service. This uncertainty also creates a demand for liquidity.[6]

While the estate tax must normally be paid within nine months of the decedent's death, there are provisions that permit the tax to be paid over ten or fifteen years. To qualify for the ten-year period, an estate must be such that the value of the farm or closely held business exceeds 35 percent of the adjusted gross estate. To qualify for the fifteen-year period, the value must exceed 65 percent of the adjusted gross estate. In the past, the provision for deferred payment had little impact because it required the executor to assume personal responsibility for all future tax payments, regardless of what happened to the value of the estate's assets in the interim. The 1976 act removes this personal responsibility in instances when the executor furnishes a bond covering the amount of deferred tax. Moreover, interest on the deferred tax is to accumulate at only 4 percent. It seems clear that the liquidity problems of closely held businesses will be somewhat alleviated by these new provisions.

---

[5] Chelcie C. Bosland, "Has Estate Taxation Induced Recent Mergers?" *National Tax Journal*, vol. 16 (June 1963), pp. 159-68. For earlier assessments that reached the same conclusions, see Harold M. Somers, "Estate Taxes and Business Mergers," *Journal of Finance*, vol. 13 (May 1958), pp. 201-10; and Wilbur A. Steger, "The Taxation of Unrealized Capital Gains and Losses: A Statistical Study," *National Tax Journal*, vol. 10 (September 1957), pp. 266-81.

[6] Tax liability also depends upon random fluctuations in stock prices. Because stock prices are sometimes subject to considerable fluctuation over short periods of time, estates composed of identical holdings of stock may carry significantly different valuations because of a few days' difference in the time of death. See C. Lowell Harriss, "Stock Prices, Death Tax Revenues, and Tax Equity," *Journal of Finance*, vol. 5 (September 1950), pp. 257-69.

Generation-Skipping Trusts

Prior to the Tax Reform Act of 1976, trusts could be used to reduce the amount of tax levied upon the devolution of an estate.[7] In light of these former rules, consider two different ways of transferring the same estate from father to son to grandson. In the first case, the father transfers $1 million to his son, who in turn claims only the interest income and transfers the remainder to the grandson. The father's estate pays a tax of $325,700 (assuming again for convenience that all figures are taxable amounts), which leaves $674,300 to the son. The son's estate of $674,300 is taxed $206,705 as it passes to the grandson. The total tax bill on the devolution of the estate from the father to the grandson via the son has been $532,405.

In the second case, the father transfers the $1 million in trust to the grandson, giving the son life tenancy of the income from the estate. The father's estate again pays a tax of $325,700, which leaves $674,300 in trust for the grandson. While the son again lives off the interest income from $674,300, no tax is levied upon his death. The grandson now receives $674,300; thus, the generation-skipping trust has reduced the tax liability on the devolution of the estate by $206,705. Yet the two cases are identical in all essential respects.

By making the tax liability depend merely on the form of transfer, trusts have been accused of generating horizontal inequity. By creating a life tenancy rather than bequeathing the corpus, it has also been argued, trusts might retard the dissipation of large holdings of wealth, reduce risk taking, and retard the rate of capital mobility.

Amid the concern expressed over generation-skipping trusts, it is important to remember that trusts serve important functions. Indeed, the primary use of trusts is not to reduce tax but to carry out these other functions. After all, trusts arose long before the introduction of estate taxation, and it cannot be claimed that they are essentially a vehicle for tax reduction. There is no doubt that they make some tax reduction possible, but that is not their purpose. The primary purpose of trusts was and is to promote the legitimate interests and concerns of donors. Newspapers are sometimes used to spank dogs, but that is not their primary function, and few would advocate discouraging newspapers in order to reduce the incidence

---

[7] For an extensive survey of trusts and their relation to estate taxation, see Gerald R. Jantscher, *Trusts and Estate Taxation* (Washington, D.C.: Brookings Institution, 1967).

of dog spanking. Moreover, to maintain a sense of perspective, it should be noted that the magnitudes involved are relatively small. Using Internal Revenue Service special tabulations for millionaire decedents, Robert Anthoine found that about 11 percent of gross transfers skipped one generation and about 3 percent skipped more than one generation.[8] Generation-skipping trusts are far from being the dominant means of passing on estates.

Prior to the 1976 act, many proposals for the taxation of trusts were advanced.[9] This act established a method of taxation that essentially treats trusts as nonexistent for tax purposes. That is, the life tenant is treated as if he owns the estate. When he dies, therefore, a tax is levied upon the trust corpus, with the net estate then being distributed to the remainderman. In the illustration given above, the death of the son is treated under the 1976 law as if the son had title to the trust corpus of $674,300 and the appropriate tax is assessed before the net estate passes to the grandson.

Federal-State Concurrent Taxation

In addition to the federal estate and gift taxes, forty-nine states levy inheritance or estate taxes and twelve levy gift taxes. Considerable complexity is sometimes created in tax compliance as a result. A person who maintains a part-time residence in a second state may be claimed as a resident by both states for death-tax purposes. Or shares of corporation stock may be taxed both by the state in which the decedent was domiciled and the state in which the corporation is chartered. Such possibilities for overlapping taxation place a cost on individuals by inducing them to conduct their affairs so as to avoid such double taxation.

Many people feel that the diversity in state death-tax laws introduces excessive complexity into tax compliance. This has led to the suggestion that greater uniformity among the states is a desirable objective of federal policy on death taxation. The simplest way of attaining this objective is to have federal preemption of death taxation.[10] Instead of federal preemption, some people suggest that

---

[8] Robert Anthoine, "Testamentary Trusts," in Carl S. Shoup, *Federal Estate and Gift Taxes* (Washington, D.C.: Brookings Institution, 1966), pp. 162-63.

[9] For a description of six alternative proposals, see A. James Casner, "American Law Institute Federal Estate and Gift Tax Project," *Tax Law Review*, vol. 22 (May 1967), pp. 576-81.

[10] See, for example, Shoup, *Federal Estate and Gift Taxes*, pp. 84-85.

the federal credit for state-death-tax payments be used more strenuously to promote greater uniformity among states.[11]

The federal credit for state death taxes appeared with the Revenue Act of 1924 and was set at a rate of 25 percent. The rate of credit was increased to 80 percent with the enactment of the Revenue Act of 1926. With the passage of the Revenue Act of 1932, which increased federal-estate-tax rates considerably, the rate of credit was maintained at 80 percent, but only 80 percent of what would have been estate-tax liability under the Revenue Act of 1926. This peculiar subterfuge continued until the Revenue Act of 1954 brought the credit into conformity with prevailing practice; the amounts of credit were not changed, but the computation was based upon prevailing death-tax schedules rather than on those enacted in 1926.

The federal credit for state-death-tax payments could be modified to encourage greater uniformity in state death taxation. To this end the Advisory Commission on Intergovernmental Relations (ACIR) recommended a three-part reform of the federal credit.[12] First, it recommended a two-bracket credit: a credit of 80 percent would be allowed on the first $250,000 of taxable estate and 20 percent on the remainder. Second, the ACIR recommended that the credit be given only for the estate type of death tax. Third, it recommended that the states be required to practice revenue maintenance for the following five years by certifying that its own death-tax collections were not reduced to offset the additional credit.

The credit device could be used even more strenuously to encourage uniformity, beyond the proposal to give credit only for estate-type taxes. More detailed specification of the format of the estate tax would be possible. The base of the state's tax that would be eligible for credit could be specified. The most complete instance of federally imposed uniformity would result from a tax supplement, under which a state simply makes its death-tax collections some percentage of the decedent's federal tax liability by a supplement of the federal estate tax. In this way the federal government would exercise considerable control over the form of state death taxation, and such control might

---

[11] See the report of the Advisory Commission on Intergovernmental Relations, *Coordination of State and Federal Inheritance, Estate, and Gift Taxes* (Washington, D.C.: 1961); and James A. Maxwell's discussion of it, "A New Proposal for Coordination of Death Taxation," *National Tax Journal*, vol. 14 (December 1961), pp. 382-87.

[12] Advisory Commission on Intergovernmental Relations, *Coordination*, pp. 16-21.

serve as the first step toward federal preemption of death taxation.[13]

Support for federal preemption of death taxes is based upon a desire to eradicate instances of overlapping taxation by two or more states. Some who take this position suggest that the federal government should share with the states the revenues they preempt, while others do not. In either event, this consideration is an incidental matter, for the case for federal preemption seems flimsy. In the first place, double taxation is the exception, not the rule. Federal preemption is a steep price to pay for avoiding a few cases of double taxation. Most cases of double taxation can be handled adequately through the legal system. At one time the Supreme Court had specified a relatively simple set of standards to govern state death taxation: realty and tangible property would be taxed in the state of location and intangible property would be taxed in the state of domicile.[14] By refusing to assign single domiciliary for tax purposes, the Court has since backed away from this principle, thereby contributing to the increased complexity of state death taxation over the past thirty years. At the same time, however, it seems clear that legal modifications can contribute to simplicity in state death taxation. Moreover, even should the law permit double taxation, it is not clear that serious problems are created so long as prospective decedents are aware of the law. Since the problems that may arise with multiple domiciliary, for instance, are well known, prospective decedents have the opportunity to arrange their affairs to avoid double taxation.

Human beings tend to seek order, and one set of tax provisions is more orderly than fifty-one. But this is a line of argument that is true for anything, whether it be tax laws, brands of cereal, styles of clothing, or news stories. Uniformity in tax institutions, as uniformity elsewhere, is purchased at a price. The price of federal preemption seems steep, especially since the alleged benefits are small and the problems can be handled in other ways.[15]

---

[13] Maxwell, "Proposal for Coordination," suggested that it would be desirable to use the federal credit to promote greater uniformity among the states as a first step toward attaining the ultimate goal of complete federal jurisdiction over transfer taxation.

[14] William J. Shultz and C. Lowell Harriss, *American Public Finance*, 8th ed. (Englewood Cliffs, N.J.: Prentice-Hall, 1965), pp. 377-78.

[15] For a good description of credits, supplements, and intergovernmental agreements as alternative ways of securing greater uniformity in state death taxation, see William H. Sager, "Practicability of Uniform Death and Gift Tax Laws," *National Tax Journal*, vol. 10 (December 1957), pp. 361-69.

7
CONTENDING TAX PRINCIPLES

The past four chapters have explored a number of issues that have surfaced regarding the current system of estate taxation. Estate taxation itself, however, cannot be taken for granted. Granted that a transfer of wealth from A to B and C is to give rise to a tax liability, we can ask whether the tax should be levied upon the amount that A bequeaths or upon the amounts that B and C inherit. This distinction defines the two contrasting forms of death taxation: estate taxation and inheritance taxation. Moreover, there is a third possibility: if transfers are defined as income, they can be taxed within a system of income taxation. The Income Tax Act of 1894, for instance, proposed to incorporate gifts and inheritances into the definition of personal income. This chapter examines these three different principles that might inform the taxation of transfers of wealth.

The Estate Principle and the Unification of Transfer Taxation

Prior to the Tax Reform Act of 1976, gifts made before death were taxed at marginal rates that were only 75 percent of the rates that would have been applied had the wealth been transferred after death. Between two people who transferred the same amount of wealth to successors, the one who made the more intensive use of gifts would have paid less tax. In consequence, it would seem that he would have been able to transfer a greater amount of wealth net of tax to his successors. To illustrate, consider two transferors, each of whom had wealth of $1,244,275 to be transferred, and ignore the computational complications that would have arisen because the two tax forms had different exemption structures. Transferring the wealth by bequest would have created a tax bill of $420,967.25, which would have left a net transfer of $823,307.75. Transferring the same amount of wealth by gift, however, would have created a tax bill of only $244,275, which would have left a net transfer of $1 million. This arithmetical example illustrates the general point that as transferors made relatively larger use of gifts, they were able to transfer larger amounts of wealth to successors.

It was argued by many persons that this difference in tax treatment between gifts and bequests violated horizontal equity, the principle that persons equally situated should pay equal amounts of tax.[1] The unification of the estate and gift taxes under the 1976 act was supported primarily because it was felt that the former system gave unwarranted favorable treatment to gifts. As the tax is now constituted, a single rate, bracket, and exemption schedule apply to all transfers of wealth made by any transferor. The value of a donor's gifts is cumulated over his lifetime, and the value of the estate is added to the value of the gifts to determine the total amount of taxable transfers.[2]

Although the view that the favorable tax treatment of gifts violates horizontal equity is widely held, there are strong grounds for suggesting that horizontal equity requires that gifts be taxed less heavily than bequests, if transfers are to be taxed at all. In the previous chapter, we saw that two tax payments made at different points in time cannot be compared adequately simply by comparing the dollar amounts of tax. The same is true for a comparison of the relative tax liabilities associated with gifts and bequests. A gift tax is paid at the time of the gift. If the wealth is held until death, the tax is paid at a later date. Transferring wealth by bequest rather than by gift makes it possible to postpone the payment of tax. To put it differently, making a gift and paying a tax, rather than leaving a bequest and then paying tax, is much like paying a bill earlier than necessary. A discount might seem in order.

To assume that a unified transfer tax is preferable to the present system of separate taxation of bequests and gifts is to assume that a

---

[1] E. G. Horsman, "The Avoidance of Estate Duty by Gifts *Inter Vivos*," *Economic Journal*, vol. 85 (September 1975), pp. 516-30.

[2] In March 1975, Great Britain put into effect a unified transfer tax. With relatively small transfers excepted, a single tax is levied on the cumulative lifetime transfers of a donor. The exception applies to cumulative transfers below £300,000. When transfers are less than £80,000, gifts are taxed only one-half as heavily as transfers at death. Beyond £80,000, the gift rate approaches the bequest rate, and the two rates become equal at £300,000. See J. F. Chown, "Capital Transfer Tax in the United Kingdom," *Canadian Tax Journal*, vol. 23, no. 5 (1975), pp. 494-500.

person who transfers $1 million during his life and $1 million upon his death should pay the same amount of tax as one who transfers $2 million upon his death and that both should pay the same tax as one who transfers $2 million during his life. While this argument might seem reasonable if interest rates were zero, it is clearly unreasonable when interest rates are positive. Compare a transfer of $2 million during life with one of $2 million upon death ten years later. Because the tax payment is made ten years earlier in the case of the *inter vivos* gift than with the bequest, the present value of the tax payment is larger for the gift than for the bequest. This divergence in present values reflects the ten years of interest that could have been earned had the tax been postponed until death. If equal transfers of wealth are to be assigned the same present value of tax liability regardless of the timing of the transfer, *inter vivos* gifts must be taxed at a lower rate than transfers upon death. The taxation of gifts at lower nominal rates than bequests would seem to be a necessary consequence of horizontal equity, not a violation of it.[3]

The Inheritance Principle and Accessions Taxation

Inheritance taxation assigns tax liability according to the amount received by heirs. Given that a separate tax is to be imposed on wealth transfers, inheritance taxation is the opposite of estate taxation. Those who favor the inheritance principle over the estate principle, while feeling that gifts should be taxed at the same rate as bequests, generally support the unification for tax purposes of gifts and bequests, only with the tax liability based on the amounts received by transferees rather than on the amounts given by transferors. This combination of an inheritance tax and a gift tax on the donee is referred to as an accessions tax and has as a base an individual's total lifetime acquisitions through gifts and inheritances.[4]

Proponents of accessions taxation argue that the amount an indi-

---

[3] On some of these matters, see Harold M. Hochman and Cotton M. Lindsay, "Taxation, Interest, and the Timing of Inter-Generational Wealth Transfers," *National Tax Journal*, vol. 20 (June 1967), pp. 219-26; and Eli Schwartz and J. Richard Aronson, "The Preference for Accumulation vs. Spending: Gift and Estate Taxation and the Timing of Wealth Transfers," *National Tax Journal*, vol. 22 (September 1969), pp. 390-98.

[4] Accessions taxation is described and examined in William D. Andrews, "The Accessions Tax Proposal," *Tax Law Review*, vol. 22 (May 1967), pp. 589-633. For a comparison of the estate and the inheritance principles of death taxation, see C. T. Sandford, *Taxing Inheritance and Capital Gains*, 2d. ed. (London: Institute of Economic Affairs, 1967), pp. 42-49.

vidual receives is a better indicator of tax-paying capacity than the amount an individual gives. What matters, according to this view, is not the size of the decedent's estate but the amounts received by individual heirs. Under accessions taxation, an estate of $1 million that was left to a sole heir would pay a larger tax on its distribution than one that was distributed equally among ten heirs. The tax extracted by a progressive accessions tax from the devolution of an estate can be reduced by increasing the number of recipients. This incentive for wider sharing is applauded by advocates of accessions taxation because they believe that some diffusion in the ownership of wealth will result.[5]

Although many people believe that basing the tax on the amount received is preferable to basing it on the amount transferred, inheritance taxation would seem to be subject to somewhat greater administrative cost than estate taxation. With an estate tax, a single value is placed on the estate and the tax is then determined. With an inheritance tax, however, a valuation must be placed on the share of each individual heir, and it is sometimes more difficult to do this than to value the total estate. It is easier, for instance, to place a single value on all household effects than first to apportion the effects among separate heirs and then to value each share. In most cases, the differences in administrative cost are insignificant, but it is never more costly to value an estate than to value the separate inheritances.

Administrative issues aside, many people argue that the size of an inheritance is a better index upon which to base tax obligations than the size of the estate from which the inheritance devolved. As with the unified transfer tax, the case for an accessions tax, as commonly promulgated, rests on the assumption that the rate of interest is zero. With a positive rate of interest, a different perspective results, though it is the reverse of the effect of a positive interest rate on a unified transfer tax. With an accessions tax, equality of present values of tax liability requires a higher rate of tax on gifts than on inheritances. The present value of a gift received today exceeds the present value of the same size inheritance to be received some time in the future. To achieve equal present values of tax liability for the different forms of transfer, it would be necessary to tax gifts more heavily than inheritances.

---

[5] The establishment of a minimum exemption per bequest, say $100,000 per legatee, would also create incentives toward wider sharing within a system of estate taxation.

The Income Principle and Transfers of Wealth

Section 102 of the Internal Revenue Code of 1954 specifically excludes from the definition of income any wealth received by gift or inheritance. In contrast, the Income Tax Act of 1894 proposed to incorporate inheritances and gifts into the definition of personal income. The primary modern advocate of treating gifts and inheritances as income is Henry Simons, who defines income as being equal to consumption plus changes in net worth.[6]

In Chapter 1, however, Simons's definition was seen to confound the important distinction between capital and income. Irving Fisher's distinction was found superior. Within the Fisherian perspective, changes in capital values are not properly defined as income, and to include such changes under an income tax would be to place a penalty upon the ownership of capital. A consistent application of this preferable definition of income would seem to preclude treating gifts or inheritances as income. Just as changes in the value of capital assets would not be income, so changes in the ownership of capital assets would not be income either. While gifts and inheritances would affect the balance sheets of the relevant persons, they would not disturb their income statements.

It is interesting to note that the proposals for incorporating gifts and inheritances into the personal income tax would do so only for the donee. The donor would not be permitted to deduct his gifts or bequests. But if gifts are to be considered income to the donee and if inheritances are to be considered income to the legatee, they should surely be considered as a loss of income to the transferor. They are considered income because they involve increases in net worth. But these increases come about only because of decreases in the net worth of the transferors.

Consider a donee whose beginning wealth was $50,000, whose consumption during the year was $15,000, and whose ending wealth was $100,000, with the increased wealth reflecting a gift of $50,000. His income for the year, under Simons's principle, is $65,000. Further suppose the donor's beginning wealth was $200,000, his consumption during the year was $40,000, and his ending wealth was $150,000, with the reduced wealth reflecting his gift of $50,000. Using Simons's

---

[6] Henry C. Simons, *Personal Income Taxation* (Chicago: University of Chicago Press, 1938), pp. 125-47. The 1966 report of the Carter commission on comprehensive tax reform in Canada recommended that gifts and inheritances be taxed as income to the recipients. See "Taxation of Income," *Report of the Royal Commission on Taxation*, vol. 3 (Ottawa: Queen's Printer, 1966), pp. 465-519.

definition of income, the donor's income is —$10,000. Consistent application of this definition of income suggests that if gifts are counted as income to the donee, they ought to be counted as losses of income to the donor. And similar principles would apply to bequests. In both cases, a logical and consistent application of Simons's definition of income would require that gifts and inheritances be treated as income to the transferees and as losses of income to the transferors.

8

INHERITANCE AND THE STATE IN A FREE AND PROSPEROUS COMMONWEALTH

Joseph Pechman is probably correct in stating that "tax theorists almost unanimously agree that estate and gift taxation should play a larger role in the revenue system."[1] Much of this acceptance of and support for transfer taxation seems to stem from reasoning based on compound interest, the permanence of capital, and a natural tendency toward cumulative inequality. This perspective leads one not only to expect the wealthy to get wealthier but also to expect the process to continue, with little chance of being reversed through the normal working of the market process. Under such circumstances, where is there to turn to but the state?

I have argued that none of these presumptions accurately describes the workings of our economic order. Nonetheless, this inaccurate vision of the nature of our economic order is that of many people, influential and otherwise. The policies that emerge from a political process informed by this false vision of our economic order portend destructive consequences for our well-being.

The Anticapitalist Mentality

Who can dispute that our economic order has been laboring increasingly under the strain of the anticapitalist mentality that was described so clearly by Ludwig von Mises?[2] This anticapitalist mentality finds expression in many forms: in the disappearance of economic due process which, in turn, led to the growth of government regulation of practically all facets of economic life; in the replacement of production by distribution as the primary economic problem of life and

---

[1] Joseph A. Pechman, *Federal Tax Policy*, rev. ed. (Washington, D.C.: Brookings Institution, 1971), p. 210.

[2] Ludwig von Mises, *The Anti-Capitalistic Mentality* (Princeton, N.J.: Van Nostrand, 1956).

focal point of political debate; in the coming of the tax state, with its highly progressive nominal-rate structure, which impinges especially heavily upon those activities that promote economic progress.

It is a well-known principle of human action that the sum of a series of momentary decisions, all of which seem desirable at the time, need not add up to a desirable pattern in the long run. This potential discord between what gets us through the immediate and what allows us to accomplish our long-range goals is something we all experience. Its resolution in different ways by different people has influenced mightily the themes of literature and the patterns of history.

In our modern political setting, we tend to resolve this eternal conflict more and more by opting for short-run, anticapitalist solutions. As time horizons shorten, as personal rates of discount rise, the character of politics and public policy changes accordingly. The redistributive emphasis of the new populism comes to command increasing attention and to find increasing expression in public policy. There is always a temptation to view the economy as a system of power relations in which economic life is essentially a struggle over who gets how much of a fixed pie, with the more numerous "have nots" fighting to overcome the "haves." Such a perspective, of course, fits in well with the new populism and serves to rationalize the sentiments it expresses. Giving vent to this sentiment, however, does not bode well if we want to stay out of the Hobbesian jungle, a jungle that these days might take on an Orwellian cast.

The economy is a system of exchange in which all gain in comparison with what their lives would be like under the Hobbesian alternative. It is not a system of power relations, a struggle over shares of a fixed pie. It is possible, of course, that unwise public policy may convert our economic life into such a struggle, as Adam Smith showed so brilliantly. The taxation of wealth is not the way to a more prosperous tomorrow. Wealth *is* our more prosperous tomorrow, and to tax it away is to destroy our future prosperity. The taxation of wealth may well make it possible to redistribute some wealth today, but it will also reduce the amount of wealth available for use tomorrow.

Inheritance and the Social Order

The maintenance of separate provisions for the taxation of wealth transfers must be supported by some argument to the effect that the source of a person's wealth is a legitimate object upon which to base differences in the tax treatment of individuals. It is sometimes suggested that "earned" wealth is more legitimate than inherited wealth,[3] though it is never said just how great athletic ability, a glib tongue, a pleasing singing voice, good looks, high intellect, or a charismatic television presence can be said to be earned. The suggestion that inherited wealth is inferior leads to proposals for the special taxation of wealth transfers. Using the jargon of modern welfare economics, if some people are "envious" of those who inherit wealth while no one is envious of those who earn their wealth, Pareto-optimality requires that this envy be assuaged via inheritance taxation.[4]

If modern welfare economics sanctions envy by proposing to build the tax system around it, this only illustrates the sterility of that discipline. To discuss inheritance within such an analytical framework is to evade most of the issues worth discussing. The acceptance of such modes of analysis precludes any analysis of the properties of a social order operating under different institutions with respect to inheritance. It would seem far more productive to focus an analysis of inheritance on the comparative properties of social orders operating with and without inheritance. When John Stuart Mill observed that the maintenance of a free society requires "liberty of tastes and pursuits . . . without impediment from our fellow-creatures, so long as what we do does not harm them, even though they should *think* our conduct foolish, perverse, or wrong,"[5] he outlined a much richer agenda concerning the institution of inheritance than can ever be derived from the analytical modes of welfare economics. As Mill saw it, the legitimization of envy was inconsistent with the maintenance of a free society; that some citizens are emotionally affronted by the choices of others must not be legitimate grounds for legislation if a free society is to survive. While Mill's prognosis may be incorrect on this point, and while there are numerous questions concerning the concrete implications of his dictum, the important point is that it establishes an altogether different agenda for examining such social institutions as inheritance, an agenda that starkly exposes the impoverishment of modern welfare economics.

---

[3] See, for example, Lester C. Thurow, *The Impact of Taxes on the American Economy* (New York: Praeger Publishers, Inc., 1971), pp. 157-58.

[4] Such an argument for using taxation to assuage envy appears in E. J. Mishan, "A Survey of Welfare Economics," *The Economic Journal*, vol. 70 (June 1960), pp. 197-256. See also Kenneth V. Greene, "Inheritance Unjustified?" *Journal of Law and Economics*, vol. 16 (October 1973), pp. 417-19.

[5] "On Liberty," in his *Utilitarianism, Liberty, and Representative Government*, Everyman's Library, No. 482 (London: Dent, 1910 [1859]), p. 75 (my italics).

The issue concerning the social function of inheritance revolves around an analysis of two alternative social orders, one operating with inheritance and one operating without. If inheritance were abolished, some envy would perhaps be assuaged. But there are also several positive features of a social order in which inheritance is sanctioned, features that would be destroyed if inheritance were abolished.

The abolition of inheritance would reduce saving and hence capital formation and economic progress, as was described in Chapter 1. As a consequence, some subtle changes would take place in our society, changes that would occur slowly but with considerable force in the long run. Without inheritance, characteristics compatible with the accumulation of wealth would have less survival value in our society relative to such characteristics as pleasing superiors, scoring well on examinations, and appearing personable in public. Hence, over time we should expect to find a reduction in those characteristics that are compatible with accumulating wealth. Yet in a free-enterprise economy, those who have become relatively wealthy are to a considerable extent those who have been relatively more successful in producing services valued highly by other people. The more a person is able to provide services that are highly valued by the recipients, the wealthier the provider will become. The characteristic of providing valuable services to others has higher survival value in a social order that permits inheritance than in one that does not, and it would seem quite important to promote the survival of this characteristic rather than to promote its extinction.[6]

Furthermore, the institution of inheritance makes possible the establishment of private sources of wealth. Therefore, inheritance makes it possible for private wealth to compete with public wealth in supporting a variety of artistic, cultural, educational, philanthropic, and scientific activities. Without competition from private wealth, government would exercise a monopoly over such areas of life. Yet the maintenance of diversity so that minority views may survive and possess a chance of becoming majority views is essential to a free society. Inheritance promotes such diversity by preventing monopoly control over the financing of such spheres of life.

Moreover, transfers of wealth reflect the existence of an affective

---

[6] For a seminal examination of the way in which an institutional framework promotes the survival of certain characteristics and not of others, see Armen A. Alchian, "Uncertainty, Evolution, and Economic Theory," *Journal of Political Economy*, vol. 58 (June 1950), pp. 211-21.

bond between transferor and transferee.[7] A legator could have purchased an annuity and left no estate but instead chose to leave an estate, reflecting the existence of an affective bond among generations. Gifts reflect such affective bonds perhaps even more strongly. What is the impact of taxing an essentially benevolent activity? One might indeed wish to tax activities that reflect hate, but why activities that reflect love? Currently, little is understood as to how social institutions induce changes in preferences. Yet social institutions seem often to have such an impact. It does not seem unreasonable to suspect that one impact of the abolition of inheritance would be to diminish intergenerational bonds, with potentially far-reaching consequences for the character of the social order.

Leaving aside possible changes in preferences, the abolition of inheritance will generate a demand for substitute institutions. Inheritance results from a demand by transferors to make transfers of wealth. The prohibition of inheritance does not diminish this demand, but rather establishes a disequilibrium, much as, for example, rent ceilings do. If the inheritance of wealth were precluded, adaptations would take place to generate other forms of inheritance in much the same manner as selling furniture to tenants and reducing the maintenance of premises are adaptations to rent ceilings. One possible adaptation to the abolition of the inheritance of wealth would be increased inheritance of occupational positions of the kind that occurs in a few labor unions. If the inheritance of positions were combined with an expanded use of employment tenure, social mobility would be retarded and caste and status would loom larger than they do now in the social order.[8]

In Summation

It seems clear that much of the support for separate provisions for transfer taxation is due to a genuine concern for assisting those who have been left out of the mainstream of American economic life. This concern would seem to imply that the primary distributional concern of our fiscal system should be to assist the unfortunate, not to penalize the fortunate. There is a fundamental difference between a tax policy designed to penalize the relatively fortunate and a tax

---

[7] Harold M. Hochman and James D. Rodgers, "Pareto Optimal Redistribution," *American Economic Review*, vol. 59 (September 1969), pp. 542-57.

[8] See, for instance, Friedrich A. Hayek, *The Constitution of Liberty* (Chicago: University of Chicago Press, 1959), p. 91.

policy designed to assist the relatively unfortunate. The present system of highly progressive rates on estates and incomes is a punitive system, pure and simple.[9] Indeed, the system seems possibly even masochistic to some degree: the penalties placed on the relatively fortunate rebound to the harm of the relatively less fortunate as well.

Attempts to penalize the fortunate through high marginal rates of tax distort the allocation of resources in several directions, creating a substantial excess burden. High marginal rates of tax reduce the willingness of investors to undertake risky investments, which decreases the rate of mobility of individuals within the distribution of income. Consequently, the wealthy are more likely to stay wealthy and the poor are less likely to become wealthy than they would otherwise be. Moreover, nominally high rates of estate taxation promote a considerable investment in estate planning to avoid tax. Not only are revenues collected by government, but also considerable investment is made in estate planning, and the investment in the latter is the deadweight loss associated with collecting the former. Taxes are collected on monetary transactions, and the higher the rate of tax the stronger the incentive to substitute in-kind transactions for monetary transactions. Equally, the higher the rate of tax, the greater the return from investing in seeking privileged tax treatment relative to the return from investing in socially productive activities. Billions of dollars are spent annually in trying to evade taxes, avoid taxes, seek out nontaxable forms of income, and secure privileged tax treatment. The amount drained off by this excess burden, which is largely generated by the highly progressive structure of nominal rates of tax, could itself promote a substantial war on poverty.

Carl Madden seems clearly to be correct when he suggests that our tax system, with its emphasis on penalizing the fruits of productive activity in the name of equalization, is making us second rate.[10] It would seem far better for nearly everyone if we stopped trying to penalize especially heavily the relatively fortunate. Such penalties are also borne in part by the relatively less fortunate. Removing the penalties would probably make nearly everyone better off. A degressive tax system without a special tax on wealth would seem to be such a system.[11] With a degressive tax, a basic level of income is exempt from tax and all income above that level is taxed

---

[9] Yeager, "Can a Liberal Be an Equalitarian?" pp. 422-40.

[10] Carl H. Madden, "Is Our Tax System Making Us Second-Rate?" *National Tax Journal*, vol. 26 (September 1973), pp. 403-7.

[11] Walter J. Blum and Harry Kalven, Jr., *The Uneasy Case for Progressive Taxation* (Chicago: University of Chicago Press, 1953), pp. 90-100.

proportionately. This form of taxation is progressive, for average rates of tax rise with income. But the focal point is the level at which tax liability begins, not the entire set of relations among all taxpayers. In other words, the emphasis is on assisting those who are relatively less fortunate rather than on penalizing those who are relatively fortunate.[12]

Within this context, inheritance is not a cause for concern. What is a cause for concern is the existence of concern about inheritance in the first place, reflecting a desire to attain distributional objectives through the use of penalties. It seems doubtful that many of us are the masochists that the intellectual effort to justify the confiscatory taxation of wealth transfers (and our many other antiproductive taxes) would appear to suggest. We are more like the person whose heating does not work and who, shivering ever more intently, holds a cigarette lighter ever closer to the thermostat. It would be far more beneficial for all of us to turn our attention, as did Adam Smith, to the profusion of neomercantilist restrictions we have set up, limiting the ability of individuals to employ their talents in whatever uses others are willing to pay them for in return. The alternative is to continue to strangle on the increasing mass of restrictions on free exchange imposed on us by the dictates of short-run political exigency. It brings to mind the Marquise de Pompadour's foreboding realization: *après nous le déluge.*

---

[12] Rather than resting content with tax exemption below some level of income, some form of income guarantee such as a negative income tax might be advocated. Financing transfer programs of this kind, however, can require the imposition of quite high marginal rates of tax even if the programs are modest in size. Edgar Browning estimated that a proposal of the National Welfare Rights Organization to guarantee an annual income of $5,500 for families of four would require marginal rates of tax of 83 percent, assuming that other government programs were unchanged, even though the total amount transferred would be only 8 percent of the net national product. Clearly, even modest efforts to achieve such guaranteed incomes can damage substantially the productive activities of our economic order. For an explanation, see Browning, *Redistribution*, pp. 96-111.

APPENDIX
Transfer Taxation in the United States

The salient features of the American system of transfer taxation as amended by the Tax Revision Act of 1976 are described in this appendix. Because it is sufficient for this purpose to present only the broad outlines of this system, I necessarily ignore or oversimplify many of the complexities of tax administration.

Federal Transfer Taxation

Liability for the federal tax on wealth transfers is computed according to the rate schedule depicted in Table A-1. The central idea of this tax is that the entire amount of a person's wealth transfers is cumulated annually and then taxed. The tax liability for any particular year is the difference between the amount of liability implied by the rate schedule and the amount of tax paid on previous transfers. To illustrate, consider a person who as of one year ago had made taxable gifts of $100,000, upon which his tax payments had been $23,800. Suppose during the current year he dies and leaves a bequest of $150,000 or, alternatively, remains alive and makes a gift of $150,000. In either event the total tax liability on $250,000 of taxable transfers is $70,800. The transferor is credited with his previous payments of $23,800, and the additional tax liability created by this current transfer is $47,000.

While this simple illustration demonstrates the central principle of the American system of transfer taxation, the actual administration of the system is considerably more complex because of the various deductions and credits that are allowed in determining just what component of gross transfers is taxable. In addition, many

Table A-1
FEDERAL TRANSFER TAX SCHEDULE

(A) Taxable transfers equal to or more than—	(B) Taxable transfers less than—	(C) Tax on amount in (A)	(D) Rate of tax on excess over amount in (A)
$ 0	$ 10,000	$	18%
10,000	20,000	1,800	20%
20,000	40,000	3,800	22%
40,000	60,000	8,200	24%
60,000	80,000	13,000	26%
80,000	100,000	18,200	28%
100,000	150,000	23,800	30%
150,000	250,000	38,800	32%
250,000	500,000	70,800	34%
500,000	750,000	155,800	37%
750,000	1,000,000	248,300	39%
1,000,000	1,250,000	345,800	41%
1,250,000	1,500,000	448,300	43%
1,500,000	2,000,000	555,800	45%
2,000,000	2,500,000	780,800	49%
2,500,000	3,000,000	1,025,800	53%
3,000,000	3,500,000	1,290,800	57%
3,500,000	4,000,000	1,575,800	61%
4,000,000	4,500,000	1,880,800	65%
4,500,000	5,000,000	2,205,800	69%
5,000,000		2,550,800	70%

Source: Internal Revenue Code of 1954, Section 2001(c).

complex issues in tax administration arise in the valuation of gifts or bequests. The valuation of real estate for local property taxation is fraught with well-known complexities, and the problems of assessing the gross value of gifts or bequests are similar. Sections 2031 through 2045 of the Internal Revenue Code, which address the valuation of gross estate, attest to the complexities of valuation, as a brief perusal would show.

Several deductions are subtracted from gross transfers to determine taxable transfers, the charitable deduction and the marital deduction being the primary ones. As a general rule, gifts or bequests to approved, tax-exempt charitable organizations are deductible from gross transfers in determining taxable transfers. Transfers to one's spouse are also generally deductible, subject to stipulated limitations. The total amount of this deduction during a transferor's lifetime cannot as a rule exceed the sum of $100,000 plus 50 percent of the amount of such transfers. Upon death, bequests to the surviving spouse may be deducted to the extent they do not exceed the greater of $250,000 or 50 percent of the adjusted gross estate, though this amount is reduced by the marital deductions taken for lifetime giving. Deductions are also allowed for the decedent's funeral expenses and the expenses of administering the estate, as well as for the decedent's unpaid debts and taxes.

After the deductions from gross estate are taken to determine taxable estate, tax liability is computed according to the schedule shown in Table A-1. Several credits are allowed against this tax liability. The most significant credit for most persons is one of $47,000 allowed for each transferor. Taxable transfers of $175,625 would carry a tax liability of $47,000, so this credit would exempt from tax this amount of taxable transfer. A credit is also allowed for state death tax payments, the rate schedule for which is shown in Table A-2. Table A-1 shows that the gross tax on a taxable estate of $1 million is $345,800. Table A-2 shows that if a state levies a tax upon either the estate or its distribution to heirs, state death tax payments up to a maximum of $36,500 can be credited against gross transfer tax. So if a state levied death taxes of $36,500 or more, the net estate tax payable to the federal government would be reduced to $309,300.

A few other forms of credit also exist. Death taxes paid to a foreign country are one. Gift taxes, paid by the decedent when the property upon which the gift tax was paid is subsequently included in the decedent's estate, are another. Also, there is a credit that occurs under the provisions for quick-succession relief. Suppose the husband predeceases the wife by, for example, one year. Without a provision for quick succession relief, the estate would be taxed once upon the husband's death and again upon the wife's death. Quick-succession relief softens the force of this double taxation of an estate. If the wife dies within two years of the husband, the wife's estate is given credit for 100 percent of her husband's estate tax payment. If the wife's death occurs within the third or fourth year following her husband's death, the credit is 80 percent of the husband's tax payment, and the credit continues to decline at 20 percent increments at each two-year interval, vanishing once the wife has survived the husband by ten years.

Besides these credits, a donor may exclude from his taxable gifts up to $3,000 per donee per year. No limit is placed on either the number of years or the number of donees. Gifts, then, enter the tax

Table A-2
FEDERAL CREDIT FOR STATE DEATH TAXES

(A) Taxable estate equal to or more than—	(B) Taxable estate less than—	(C) Credit on amount in (A)	(D) Rate of credit on excess over amount in (A)
$ 40,000	$ 90,000		0.8%
90,000	140,000	$ 400	1.6%
140,000	240,000	1,200	2.4%
240,000	440,000	3,600	3.2%
440,000	640,000	10,000	4.0%
640,000	840,000	18,000	4.8%
840,000	1,040,000	27,600	5.6%
1,040,000	1,540,000	38,800	6.4%
1,540,000	2,040,000	70,800	7.2%
2,040,000	2,540,000	106,800	8.0%
2,540,000	3,040,000	146,800	8.8%
3,040,000	3,540,000	190,800	9.6%
3,540,000	4,040,000	238,800	10.4%
4,040,000	5,040,000	290,800	11.2%
5,040,000	6,040,000	402,800	12.0%
6,040,000	7,040,000	522,800	12.8%
7,040,000	8,040,000	650,800	13.6%
8,040,000	9,040,000	786,800	14.4%
9,040,000	10,040,000	930,800	15.2%
10,040,000		1,082,800	16.0%

Source: Internal Revenue Code of 1954, Section 2011 (b).

base only to the extent that a donee receives more than $3,000 in any one year. To illustrate the impact of the annual exemption, consider three donors, each of whom makes gifts of $30,000 during the year. Let the first make a single gift of $30,000, the second three gifts of $10,000 each, and the third ten gifts of $3,000 each. After the annual per donee exemption had been subtracted, the value of taxable gifts would be $27,000 for the first donor, $21,000 for the second donor, and zero for the third.

State Transfer Taxation

All states except Nevada impose death taxes; fifteen use estate taxation and thirty-four use inheritance taxation. Twelve states, moreover, levy a gift tax. Table A-3 shows that considerable variation

Table A-3

STATE ESTATE TAX RATES

State	Marginal Rate Range (on taxable estate, in percent)	Minimum Rate Applies to:	Maximum Rate Applies above:	Specific Exemption
Alabama		Maximum federal credit		$ 60,000
Alaska	0.8–16	Maximum federal credit		60,000
Arizona		$50,000	$10,000,000	100,000
Arkansas		Maximum federal credit		60,000
Florida		Maximum federal credit		60,000
Georgia		Maximum federal credit		60,000
Mississippi	1.0–16	$60,000	10,000,000	60,000
New Mexico		Maximum federal credit		60,000
New York	2.0–21	$50,000	10,000,000	Variable
North Dakota	2.0–23	$25,000	1,500,000	20,000
Ohio	2.0– 7	$40,000	500,000	5,000
Oklahoma	1.0–10	$10,000	10,000,000	15,000
South Carolina	4.0– 6	$40,000	100,000	60,000
Utah	5.0–10	$35,000	85,000	60,000
Vermont		30% of federal estate tax		60,000

Source: *Facts and Figures on Government Finance*, 18th ed. (New York: Tax Foundation, Inc., 1975), p. 210.

exists in the rate schedules of the states that practice estate taxation. Ohio provides a specific exemption of only $5,000, while Arizona provides one of $100,000. South Carolina has a nearly proportional tax rate, as the marginal tax rate is 4 percent on the first $40,000 of taxable estate and rises to 6 percent on the value in excess of $100,000. North Dakota, by contrast, has a steeply progressive estate tax, rising from 2 percent on the first $25,000 to 23 percent on the amount of taxable estate in excess of $1.5 million.

It should be noted that Alabama, Alaska, Arkansas, Florida, Georgia, and New Mexico all duplicate the exemption and bracket structure of the federal estate tax, with their rates set equal to the maximum federal credit allowed on any given estate. And Vermont sets its tax at 30 percent of the federal estate tax liability. If a decedent in one of these states left an estate of $1,040,000, the state would claim an estate tax of $38,800, which is the full value of the federal credit (see Table A-2). Seven of the remaining nine states impose pickup taxes to ensure full absorption of the federal credit. The tax liability in two remaining states, Mississippi and North Dakota, would clearly exceed the amount of maximum federal credit.

Table A-4 shows that considerable variation also exists in the rate schedules of the thirty-four states that practice inheritance taxation. In New Jersey the rate of tax on transfers to spouse, child, or parent ranges from 1 to 16 percent, while in Virginia it ranges from 1 to 5 percent. The rate of tax on transfers to nonrelatives ranges from 10 to 30 percent in Illinois, West Virginia, and Wisconsin, while in Louisiana it ranges from 5 to 10 percent. A similar degree of variation also exists in the size of the specific exemption. Kansas, for instance, permits a specific exemption of $75,000 on transfers to the surviving spouse, while Maryland allows only $150.

Although considerable variety exists in particular rate schedules, the primary features of the inheritance tax are quite similar among the states. All states except Oregon, for instance, vary the rate of tax with consanguinity, with the rate of tax declining as the transferee's relation to the transferor becomes closer. Except for Oregon, South Dakota, and West Virginia, states that use an inheritance tax also impose a pickup tax upon the estate in the event the inheritance tax collected from the shares of the estate is too small to absorb the full amount of the federal credit. A federal taxable estate of $240,000, for instance, is allowed a maximum credit of $3,600 for state-death-tax payments. If a state collects only $2,600 in inheritance taxes from the distribution of the estate, the state would levy a pickup tax of $1,000 against the estate in order to absorb fully the federal credit.

Table A-4

STATE INHERITANCE TAX RATES AND EXEMPTIONS

State	Marginal Rate Range (in percent)			Exemptions ($ thousands)			
	Spouse, child, or parent	Brother or sister	Other than relative	Spouse	Child or parent	Brother or sister	Other than relative
California	3–14	6–20	10–24	5	5	2	0.3
Colorado	2–8	3–10	10–19	20	10	2	0.5
Connecticut	2–8	4–10	8–14	50	10	3	0.5
Delaware	1–6	5–10	10–16	20	3	1	None
Hawaii	1.5–7.5	3.5–9	3.5–9	20	5	0.5	0.5
Idaho	2–15	4–20	8–20	10	4	1	None
Illinois	2–14	2–14	10–30	20	20	10	0.1
Indiana	1–10	5–15	7–20	15	2	0.5	0.1
Iowa	1–8	5–10	10–15	40	10	None	None
Kansas	0.5–5	3–12.5	10–15	75	15	5	0.2
Kentucky	2–10	4–16	6–16	10	5	1	0.5
Louisiana	2–3	5–7	5–10	5	5	1	0.5
Maine	2–6	8–12	12–18	15	10	0.5	0.5
Maryland	1	7.5	7.5	0.15	0.15	0.15	0.15
Massachusetts	1.8–11.8	5.5–19.3	8–19.3	30	15	5	5
Michigan	2–8	2–8	10–15	30	5	5	None
Minnesota	1.5–10	6–25	8–30	30	6	1.5	0.5
Missouri	1–6	3–18	5–30	20	5	0.5	0.1
Montana	2–8	4–16	8–32	20	2	0.5	None
Nebraska	1	1	6–18	10	10	10	0.5
New Hampshire	Exempt	15	15	Unlimited	a	None	None
New Jersey	1–16	11–16	15–16	5	5	0.5	0.5
North Carolina	1–12	4–16	8–17	10	2	None	None
Oregon	2–10	2–10	2–10	Unlimited	Unlimited	3	0.5
Pennsylvania	6	15	15	None	None	None	None
Rhode Island	2–9	3–10	8–15	10	10	5	1
South Dakota	1.5–12	4–16	6–24	60	3	0.5	0.1
Tennessee	5.5–9.5	6.5–20	6.5–20	60	60	1	1
Texas	1–6	3–10	5–20	25	25	10	0.5
Virginia	1–5	2–10	5–15	5	5	2	1
Washington	1–10	3–20	10–25	10	10	1	None
West Virginia	3–13	4–18	10–30	15	5	None	None
Wisconsin	1.25–12.5	5–25	10–30	50	4	1	0.5
Wyoming	2	2	6	10	10	10	None

a Children are wholly exempt, but parents are taxed at 15 percent.
Source: *Facts and Figures on Government Finance*, 18th ed. (New York: Tax Foundation, Inc., 1975), pp. 208–9.